SEQUENCING THE PRIMARY CURRICULUM

T0368856

SEQUENCING THE
PRIMARY CURRICULUM

SEAMUS GIBBONS & EMMA LENNARD

S Sage

S Sage

1 Oliver's Yard
55 City Road
London EC1Y 1SP

2455 Teller Road
Thousand Oaks, California 91320

Unit No 323-333, Third Floor, F-Block
International Trade Tower Nehru Place
New Delhi – 110 019

8 Marina View Suite 43-053
Asia Square Tower 1
Singapore 018960

Editor: James Clark
Editorial Assistant: Esosa Otabor
Production Editor: Gourav Kumar
Copyeditor: Sharon Cawood
Proofreader: Sarah Cooke
Indexer: KnowledgeWorks Global Ltd
Marketing Manager: Lorna Patkai
Cover Design: Naomi Robinson
Typeset by KnowledgeWorks Global Ltd
Printed in the UK

Library of Congress Control Number: 2023932429

British Library Cataloguing in Publication data

A catalogue record for this book is available from the British Library

ISBN 978-1-5296-0074-2
ISBN 978-1-5296-0073-5 (pbk)

At Sage we take sustainability seriously. Most of our products are printed in the UK using responsibly sourced papers and boards. When we print overseas we ensure sustainable papers are used as measured by the Paper Chain Project grading system. We undertake an annual audit to monitor our sustainability.

Dedicated to Nicole Quaradeghini
For the teacher you were and the teacher you would have become.
With our love.

Contents

About the Authors

Seamus Gibbons is currently the Executive Principal for a number of London primary schools and the primary phase lead for the initial teacher training programme of the largest multi-academy trust in the country (which was recently graded as 'Outstanding' by Ofsted). Seamus has led schools to achieve the Ofsted 'Outstanding' rating and passionately believes in the positive foundation primary education sets for the future success of all children, regardless of background. Seamus has a Masters in Effective Learning (distinction) from the Institute of Education and has also achieved the National Qualification for Executive Leadership. He was a member of the DfE's headteacher reference group for over five years and when he is not engaged in all things education, Seamus loves to travel and see as much of the world as possible.

Emma Lennard is an independent primary curriculum advisor, working with schools across the country. She currently works with the Knowledge Schools Trust to develop the Primary Knowledge Curriculum; writing curriculum content, developing CPD for teachers and delivering training. Emma also delivers initial teacher training for a national multi-academy trust. She previously worked with the Westminster-based think-tank, Civitas, developing the Core Knowledge UK curriculum. Emma has supported DfE panels on National Professional Qualifications and Early Years. Before completing a PGCE with the Primary Catholic Partnership in Southampton and then teaching in central London, Emma worked for a member of the European Parliament in Brussels and studied International Relations at the University of Exeter. Emma lives in London with her husband and their two young boys, who frequently remind her that she still has lots to learn about the world.

Acknowledgements

We are very grateful to so many of our colleagues, friends and family who have given their time, expertise and advice throughout the process of writing this book. For all of your wisdom and support and patience, we thank you:

Caroline Ellen
Claire Knott
Alex Lennard
Robin Miller
Alex Pethick
Naomi Pilling
Juli Ryzop

How to Use this Book

This book is aimed at trainee teachers, early career teachers and teachers who are interested in primary **curriculum** design.

We have written this book so that you can dip in and out of the chapters, but we recommend reading the first section of the book including, 'What is Curriculum?', 'The National Curriculum', 'A Coherent, Sequenced Primary Curriculum' and 'Diversity and Inclusion' first. Content within these chapters will be referred to throughout the book.

At the end of each chapter, there are questions to reflect upon. These might form part of a group exercise, be used for individual study, or they might be questions you can ask experts in school guardians and carers.

The content of this book is a culmination of our experience of working as teachers and then leaders and specialists within school. We know we cannot tell you everything you need to know about the curriculum in one book – that would be an impossible task. We hope that this book will help to focus your thinking about the primary curriculum, and that you will be able to use it as a stepping stone to further your own understanding. As teachers in the early stages of your careers, you will be learning more than this book could ever teach you, but we hope to have contributed in a small way to your journey into this wonderful profession.

Do question and challenge the content of this book, read widely, establish your own understanding, and keep asking yourself if you are as close to the truth as you can be. Education is evolving and changing at a rapid pace, so we need to be adaptable, open-minded and always willing to learn. Most importantly, keep the children you teach at the centre of every decision you make; everything we do as teachers is for them.

Thank you from us both for opening this book and for your service to the children you teach.

Part 1

1

WHAT IS THE CURRICULUM?

The word **curriculum** has its roots in the Greek *khouros*, meaning run, and the Latin *currere*, meaning to run the course or move forward. The curriculum therefore enables children to move forwards on their journey of understanding. The primary curriculum outlines what children need to know and be able to do at each stage of their primary education until they leave Year 6. We know that children all have different starting points, and will progress through the curriculum at different speeds. Some children may travel through the curriculum in different ways, noticing different things, but they all follow the path we have established for them, the path we have designed and planned for, with the best of our knowledge and skills as teachers.

Primary schools have many roles and responsibilities but if we return to the core purpose of a school, it is to educate. The curriculum sets out what children should learn to become educated. It is not for us to decide what that education is for. Some people argue that we are educating children so they may find employment; you may have heard people say that we are educating children for jobs that haven't been invented yet. For some, education is about jumping through the hoops set out by examination systems, for passing SATs and GCSEs. For us, education is about freedom, freedom of thought and freedom of choice.

The curriculum needs to provide a wealth of knowledge with which children can think critically. It is impossible to think critically about something you know nothing about. If a child has learned lots about the world, they can understand what is happening in it. They can draw upon their understanding of different points in history, different world events and different ways in which people live to make sense of what is happening around them. We want our children to be free to think deeply and critically. Vitally, a child who understands the world can forge their own path through it. Knowledge and understanding can offer freedom of choice; a freedom to determine their own lives.

As teachers, we cannot change a child's circumstances. But we can provide them with a curriculum that will help children to know themselves and the people in their community and beyond. We can ensure the curriculum equips them with the vocabulary they need to communicate and to participate in the world around them. We can make a promise to the children in our care that we will help them to find, nurture and amplify their voice, because what they think and what they say matter.

The curriculum is our gift to the children in our schools and every part of it needs to contribute to their journey. Therefore, what we include in our curriculum needs to be important, beautiful and true. From the artists whose work we appreciate to the scientific concepts we grapple with, everything we include must be worthy of a place. We must consider the **inclusion** of diverse voices, ensuring the curriculum reflects the world we live in and enables children to see themselves in the authors, scientists, engineers and musicians we study. We know that over time, our understanding changes, and new discoveries are made, and so our curriculum must be adaptable. We must therefore constantly reflect and adapt to ensure the curriculum delivers the best we can possibly offer our children, so they can run free.

2

THE NATIONAL CURRICULUM

In England, maintained schools (those operating under the control of a Local Authority) must follow the **National Curriculum** as set out by the Department for Education. Free schools and Academies have the freedom to choose their own curriculum, but it must be broad and balanced. The National Curriculum outlines what should be taught in primary school in **Key Stage** 1 (years 1 and 2) and Key Stage 2 (years 3, 4, 5 and 6).

See Section 78 of the 2002 Education Act (at www.legislation.gov.uk/ukpga/2002/32/section/78). This applies to all maintained schools.

Academies are also required to offer a broad and balanced curriculum in accordance with Section 1 of the 2010 Academies Act (see www.legislation.gov.uk/ukpga/2010/32/section/1).

The **Early Years Foundation Stage** is separate from the National Curriculum. It sets out learning and development for children from 0 to 5 years old. The Early Years Foundation Stage is structured around the seven areas of learning:

- communication and language
- physical development
- personal, social and emotional development
- literacy
- mathematics
- understanding the world
- expressive arts and design.

Table 2.1   Areas of learning

Early Years Foundation Stage		National Curriculum	
Nursery	Reception	Key Stage 1	Key Stage 2
0-3 years	4-5 years	5-7 years	7-11 years

When children move from reception into Year 1, they are transitioning between the Early Years Foundation Stage and the National Curriculum. Schools often have a plan in place to support children with this transition.

The National Curriculum states that every school must offer a curriculum which:

- promotes the spiritual, moral, cultural, mental and physical development of pupils at the school and of society, and
- prepares pupils at the school for the opportunities, responsibilities and experiences of later life. (DfE, 2013a: 5)

The Primary National Curriculum in England includes the following subjects:

- English
- Mathematics
- Science
- History
- Geography
- Art
- Music
- Physical Education
- Computing
- Design Technology
- Physical, Social, Health and Emotional Education (PSHE).

Religious Education (RE) is a statutory subject (schools are legally obliged to teach it) but specific subject content is not included in the National Curriculum. Schools often follow a locally agreed programme for RE. Faith schools such as Catholic institutions may follow their own programme linked to their denomination. Within the National Curriculum, English, maths and sometimes science are known as 'core' subjects. The other subjects are known as 'foundation' subjects.

The National Curriculum forms one part of a school curriculum; it is not the total curriculum a school will offer. Other experiences, trips, enrichment activities and activities based on need and local context will contribute to an individual school's curriculum.

The National Curriculum outlines what should be taught in each subject but does not suggest how it should be taught. For example, the music curriculum for

Key Stage 1 states: 'Pupils should be taught to use their voices expressively and creatively by singing songs and speaking chants and rhymes' (DfE, 2013b).

This curriculum guidance stipulates that children must be taught to sing songs, but it does not specify which songs, in which sequence, or to what standard of performance. It is left to the individual school to decide how this is taught. Often, schools follow schemes of work, programmes that provide much more detail for teachers. A scheme of work may provide individual lesson plans that, if followed, will enable children to meet what is set out in the National Curriculum. In some cases, individual teachers plan units of work using the aims from the National Curriculum and add their own content. The National Curriculum provides information about what needs to be taught, but teachers need to do some important thinking and decision making to construct their own school curriculum.

Some schools organise their curriculum by subject, so you would see subjects such as science and history timetabled. Some schools organise their curriculum into topics, in what is known as a 'cross-curricular' approach. Within a topic, a broad umbrella name such as 'under the sea' is given and, within that, a teacher would teach a bit of history, geography, science and art. Some schools do a mixture of the two – for example, they might teach subjects but merge history, geography and art into topics. The challenge of a cross-curricular or topic-based approach is that children may not know they are learning history or geography, so they may not grasp disciplinary understanding. If children are making bread whilst learning about the Anglo-Saxons, they may confuse the activity with the discipline of history. Making bread is a worthwhile and valuable activity for many reasons and might feature in the cooking part of the design technology curriculum. However, if a child thinks 'We made bread in history today!' then they might be developing misconceptions about the identity of the discipline of history.

There is no single model of a perfect primary curriculum. There are many different approaches and much debate over both content and delivery of the primary school curriculum. This is a good thing. A school curriculum should be constantly reviewed, adapted and improved, all to meet the needs of the children the school serves. The world changes, our own understanding of the world changes, and our school curriculum should change to reflect this reality. During our careers, it is highly likely that the National Curriculum will change; priorities, political or otherwise, might result in content changes. So, therefore, we must, over time, develop a sense of what the curriculum means to us as teachers, what we value, what we believe in. In everything we do, we must always bring our thinking back to the children we teach, because their education is precious, and we are responsible for it.

QUESTIONS TO ASK EXPERTS

- Do we teach subjects discretely or do we teach cross-curricular topics?
- Do we use any schemes of work?
- How do we teach foundation subjects?
- How does our school curriculum deliver the National Curriculum?

3

A COHERENT, SEQUENCED PRIMARY CURRICULUM

So far, we have thought about the purpose of the primary curriculum and we have looked at the structure of the National Curriculum. Within this chapter, we are going to consider the following:

- **Coherence**: what does it mean and what does it look like?
- **Sequencing**: how and why do we need to sequence our primary curriculum?

Coherence is the quality of something that is logical and consistent. Simply put, a coherent curriculum makes sense. This sounds obvious, but in many schools, the curriculum has developed over time, been added to by different people at different points with different knowledge and skills. This can work, however, without oversight, the curriculum can become piecemeal, fractured and inconsistent. Year 4 might 'do Rivers' because they've always done Rivers, not because it builds on their prior knowledge or prepares them for future learning. Rather than 'doing Rivers', an important conversation could be had to ask, why this, why now? It might be that Year 4 is the right place for Rivers because it builds on learning from Year 3, prepares them for future learning in Year 5 and links to other subject areas such as the Water

Cycle in Science. Understanding these reasons is important so that you know what you are teaching and why. Within a coherent curriculum, everything is there for a reason; it makes sense.

The primary curriculum is never something that is done or finished. It is a constantly adapting, evolving and living thing. That said, the primary curriculum needs to be strong, it needs to have structure and it needs to be very clear. We need to know what our children need to learn and in what order. Deciding what order we teach content in is called *sequencing* and is the focus of this book. A sequence of learning sets out what children need to know in a deliberately structured order. We sequence primary curriculum content to help children learn it well. If we do not sequence curriculum content, it can become muddled, episodical, mixed up. Children might have a lovely time learning lots of different things about Ancient Egypt, but if the content does not fit into a well-planned sequence, their knowledge and understanding will not build over time. Table 3.1 is an example of an *incoherent* history and geography curriculum that has evolved with little oversight.

Table 3.1   An incoherent curriculum

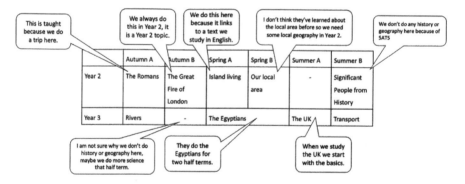

You can see from this example that even with the best of intentions, a curriculum can lack coherence. What it is vital to do is to take a step back and think about *why* we do what we do. Sequencing our curriculum helps us to focus on the order we teach things in. This helps to make the curriculum coherent. Table 3.2 is an example of a *coherent* history and geography curriculum map that has been carefully planned.

These two examples show the power of careful curriculum thinking. We need to make sure we know why we are teaching what we are teaching and ask ourselves, does this all make sense?

A coherent, sequenced primary curriculum is a powerful one. It is powerful because, if designed well, a curriculum can help children to learn more and remember more over time. Remembering is something that we need to think carefully

Table 3.2 A coherent curriculum

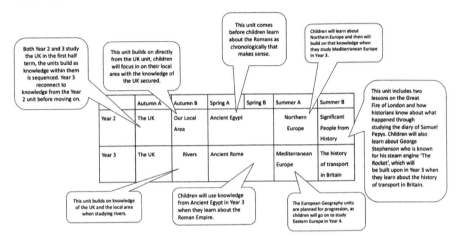

about when we sequence our curriculum. When will children be expected to remember what we have taught them?

The example below illustrates how a primary child's understanding of democracy could develop within a coherent, well-sequenced curriculum where school leaders have planned the curriculum thoughtfully.

Example: Conceptual Understanding of Democracy

Early years: Children share books about kings and queens, and role-play characters from familiar stories. They may learn about important landmarks of the UK, flags and countries of the UK through storytelling, cultural celebrations, trips and visitors. They might talk about voting in elections, particularly if the school is used as a polling station. Early understanding of democracy may start with understanding how the school council works, or with the teacher explaining that we can count how many people have chosen something:

> So, reception, we can either read The Smartest Giant in Town or The Hungry Caterpillar. Let's have a vote to find out which book most people would prefer. Put your hand up if you'd prefer this book … OK, that is ten people and now put your hand up if you'd prefer this book … I see 15 hands up! So which book got the most votes? Some of you might feel disappointed because your book isn't the one we will read right now. When we vote, sometimes our choice isn't the most popular; it doesn't get the most votes. Voting helps us to find the most popular choice, but it may not be something everyone has chosen.

Key Stage 1: Children learn more about kings and queens and progress with their understanding by looking at leaders. They may look at important landmarks or buildings, such as the Houses of Parliament in art. They may learn about significant people from the past, such as King John who sealed the Magna Carta. This may be taught through storytelling, role play or by engaging with a text. When studying the Magna Carta, children are developing ideas about power, resistance, promises and justice, all of which will contribute to their understanding of democracy:

'Year 2, why did the Barons ask King John to agree with the promises in the Magna Carta?'

'The Barons wanted to stop King John doing unfair things like putting people in prison and taking too much tax money.'

'That is right, they stood up to King John and told him that even though he was the King, he needed to behave in a fair way.'

Key Stage 2: Children learn many different examples of how societies have been ruled in the past, including Ancient Egypt and the Pharaohs, Ancient Rome and the Emperors. They may study Ancient Greece and the development of *democracy* (from the Greek *demos*, meaning people, and *kratia*, meaning power). They may learn that the adult male citizens of Greece were expected to participate in voting. This may raise questions about who is eligible for voting and children may go on to learn about the Suffragette movement in England. Throughout KS2, children will encounter many different people and periods of time. As their understanding of democracy grows, they will be able to talk about power, resistance, promises and justice, and how at different times democracy has flourished or been threatened. This will prepare them well for secondary school and for understanding the world around them.

To summarise:

- A coherent curriculum is one that makes sense; it is clear how and why it has been designed.
- Sequencing the curriculum involves thinking about the order of the content so that knowledge can grow over time.

QUESTIONS TO CONSIDER

- How is my content within a subject sequenced?
- What prior knowledge will children need for each unit and when did they learn it?

- How are my units linked to one another within this subject?
- How are my units linked to other subject areas?
- What forthcoming units are linked to these units I am teaching? (Are they in the next year, the next key stage?)
- Does the sequencing of my curriculum make sense?

4

DIVERSITY AND INCLUSION

The National Curriculum document outlines the core content primary schools need to teach. It is up to schools to add the detail, to decide how they sequence the materials so that they build knowledge in small steps, to make the pedagogical choices needed to deliver the curriculum, and to choose the individual contexts and materials the school will use to bring the curriculum to life. Schools bring the curriculum to children, so we must think about the children we are serving.

Whilst this book is primarily about sequencing and knowing the requirements of each discipline, we feel it is essential for new teachers to reflect upon diversity and inclusion. It is important to always consider how a curriculum will mirror the diverse population our children live within in this country.

We live in communities that may have a range of different languages, ethnic groups, religious beliefs, disabilities, sexual orientations, and family set-ups. It is important that our children see themselves within the curriculum they are learning. Carefully selecting content which reflects this is an important part of curriculum development. When we make curriculum choices, we are telling a story. As teachers, we may not realise it, but we hold power; the power to decide what story we tell our children about the world we live in. Not only should we consider the essential people, places, processes and events that children must learn about, but we need to also ask, whose voices are left unheard? Why are many of the famous scientists in history male? What prevented women from achieving the same successes at the time? Are people from black and global majority communities underrepresented in our school curriculum? Through our curriculum choices, we can ensure that children in our schools learn about the achievements of a diverse range of people.

Consider, for a moment, the power of a young child seeing an astronomer in a science lesson that looks like them, who perhaps has the same skin colour, speaks the same language, has a disability. What message does this send to that child?

As we design a curriculum, at top level, some questions we should be reflecting on are as follows:

- What does a child working through our curriculum see?
- Who are the significant people we study?
- Do pupils see diverse role models from different ethnic backgrounds?
- Are we reflecting on our own unconscious biases?
- Are people with special needs and disabilities represented positively?
- Does the curriculum challenge gender stereotypes?
- How are different family set-ups and members of the LGBTQ+ community represented?
- How do children see themselves within the curriculum?

There is much literature available to support schools in ensuring that their school curriculum represents diversity and inclusion, however below we have provided some specific examples of content from the National Curriculum for you to reflect on, using some of the questions below. The questions and reflections are transferable to different subjects.

Art and Design

The art and design curriculum requires children to learn about great artists, architects and designers, and this is a good opportunity for us to consider which individuals we teach the children about.

Reflection questions

- Do the artists, architects and designers selected reflect a range of different ethnic backgrounds?
- Are there any local people who reflect the local community who could be included in the curriculum? Or if the local community is not very diverse, how will you broaden children's knowledge of diversity in these areas of art and design?
- Do you openly teach about some of the barriers these people faced in their lives? For example, is an artist struggling with mental health issues?
- Is there a local architect who can come and speak to the children?

Computing

The computing curriculum requires us to teach children about algorithms, coding and e-safety. It is possible to teach these aspects of the curriculum without including a thread of diversity and inclusion, but we know that girls are less likely to study STEM when they are older and that those from disadvantaged backgrounds do not always have access to the same computing resources as those enjoying greater affluence at home. Therefore, it is essential that these children see themselves within the computing curriculum.

Reflection questions

- Are there posters/visuals of women in computing for children to see? Can you invite some females who work in technology to inspire and speak to the children?
- When teaching e-safety, are the resources reflective of a range of individuals? Does the curriculum consider how those with a special need may face unique difficulties depending on their need? Are you ensuring that the materials used to teach these lessons do not represent one type of person as being the wrongdoer in the scenarios presented?

Design and Technology

In the design and technology (D&T) curriculum, we are required to teach cooking and nutrition as one element. This provides us with the opportunity to introduce children to cuisines and traditions from around the world. We can also consider some designers and engineers that children may come across when looking at D&T.

Reflection questions

- Which chefs have you introduced to the children? How do they reflect diversity?
- Which ingredients are used for cooking? Which countries do these come from?
- Are there local restaurants or parents/carers within the school community who the school can engage with?
- Which designers, engineers or technology specialists do children encounter in the curriculum?

English

At the heart of the English curriculum is developing a love of reading, and we should consider carefully how our reading curriculum represents diversity and inclusion.

Reflection questions

- Which picture books do you use within your school and as part of your curriculum? Do they represent a range of different cultures, ethnic backgrounds, family set-ups, and people with disabilities? Do we ever risk telling a single story? For example, *Handa's Surprise* by Eileen Browne is a popular choice in the early years, however could children develop the misconception that all African children live in small villages? How do we counter this whilst still sharing this lovely story?
- Which poets and authors have been chosen for texts in the curriculum? Do they represent a range of different writers? Does the school library/reading area in the school exemplify diversity?
- Is there a sufficient and diverse range of non-fiction books which represent a wide range of inspiring people? Countries and places of the world? A range of religions?

Geography

Pupils develop their locational knowledge across the KS1 and KS2 curriculum – they need to know the different continents and locate the world's countries. This is a great opportunity for us to reflect on what our children already know about the cultures and world they live in, and about how our geography curriculum can expand their knowledge.

Reflection questions

- What locational knowledge does your curriculum develop? Does it represent a range of places? Do children get to compare where they live with a range of different locations?
- When choosing field study/locations to visit, do children visit diverse places which will broaden their knowledge of the wider world?

History

Just as in art and design, in history we want children to learn about significant individuals in this discipline. In KS2, we are also required to teach children about a non-European society.

Reflection questions

- Which significant people have we included in our history curriculum? Are they all white or Western? Does the curriculum include how these significant individuals have shaped our world today?
- How is black history threaded through your curriculum? How do you ensure it is not just a one-off event and that it is something which is meaningfully integrated?
- What non-European society features within your history curriculum? How does this broaden your children's knowledge?
- Does your curriculum teach about colonialism? Does it avoid teaching that places were 'discovered' when there were already people living there, just not white British people?

Maths

The maths curriculum focuses on our children developing their reasoning, problem solving and fluency as they progress through the primary curriculum. Whilst there is no direct requirement to teach about individuals, there is still an opportunity to naturally weave elements of diversity into the maths curriculum.

Reflection questions

- Do the word problems or reasoning presented to children naturally reference a diverse range of people? For example, they could reference a child having two mothers; someone visiting a Mosque; the circumference of a wheelchair wheel; a range of different names, etc.
- When discussing the importance of maths in the real world, does the curriculum link with some significant mathematicians who reflect diversity in the subject?
- If your school has a maths or enterprise week, what speakers could the school bring in who will reflect inclusion and diversity?

Music

There is explicit reference in the music curriculum to children learning music from a range of musicians and various traditions. It is important that we sequence this, so that children are exposed to a range of different musicians as well as to music from different cultures. It is important that we, as teachers, avoid making presumptions that certain groups of children will not like a particular style of music, and instead provide them with the opportunity to experience and learn the breadth of the music world.

Reflection questions

- Which musicians do children learn about and hear in the music curriculum? Are the choices we have made diverse?
- What musical traditions are shared with children? Do they reflect the wider world?
- Do children get exposed to and learn to value a range of music from different countries and cultures?

Physical Education

As part of the PE curriculum, we need to teach a range of competitive sports. It is at school level that we can carefully choose what sports we teach and the significant sporting individuals who inspire these sports. This is the perfect subject to challenge stereotypes around only girls being good at dance or football being a male-only sport. We can also find inspiration in the wide range of excellent Paralympians and record breakers from all countries around the world.

Reflection questions

- When playing a range of sports is there a deliberately planned opportunity to tackle potential stereotypes?
- Are a range of sports people used to inspire the children in different sports? Do children see people who look like them playing the different sports we teach?
- How do we ensure we have selected sports which all children can access – for example, how will a child in a wheelchair access these sports?

The above provides some examples of how we can reflect upon each discipline through the lens of diversity and inclusion. We can use these reflection questions to support us in a range of different subjects.

An important aspect of this is that the diversity and inclusion elements of our curriculum are authentic and not a bolt on to our curriculum offer. Diversity and inclusion should be woven meaningfully through the curriculum, and we should continue to reflect upon it to ensure we are doing the best we can to reflect the world our children live in today.

Religious Education

Whilst there is not an agreed curriculum for religious education, it is still important we have a critical lens when developing an RE curriculum or purchasing a particular scheme. There is a requirement that the RE teaching in the curriculum has a higher proportion of Christianity, but this subject is key to developing tolerance of all beliefs. In school, we are required to promote 'fundamental British values' and at the heart of this is tolerance for different beliefs.

Reflection questions

- When do children encounter different religions in the curriculum? Do they get to learn about their religion in KS1? If not, what is the rationale for this?
- Are there trips planned to all places of worship? If it is not possible to get to a particular place of worship, how is this countered? Is a visitor invited in? Could technology allow for a virtual tour?
- What about those who do not have a specific religion – how are their views and beliefs included in the curriculum sensitively?

Signposts to Additional Resources

Useful links to read more around diversity in the curriculum:

- Black Curriculum – https://theblackcurriculum.com
- Diverse Educators – www.diverseeducators.co.uk/diversifying-the-curriculum-a-perspective
- Karin Doull – *Teaching a Diverse Primary Curriculum* (Exeter: Learning Matters, 2022)
- Promoting fundamental British values as part of spiritual, moral, social and cultural development (SMSC) in school – www.gov.uk/government/publications/promoting-fundamental-british-values-through-smsc

Part 2

5

EARLY READING

This chapter will outline

- Why early reading is so important
- Phonics
- Key elements of an early reading curriculum
- How to build your own subject knowledge
- Signposts to additional resources

Why Early Reading Is so Important

Early reading is not a subject on its own – it forms part of the English curriculum content for KS1 and KS2, and part of the Literacy content of the statutory framework for the Early Years Foundation Stage. However, it is such a key part of children's early learning that we felt it was necessary to include a chapter dedicated to early reading.

There is a clear expectation, set out in the Core Content Framework, that trainee teachers should learn that *systematic synthetic phonics is the most effective approach for teaching pupils to decode*. The statutory Teachers' Standards (DfE, 2011) also stress the expectation that teachers have a secure understanding of phonics when teaching early reading.

So why is there such an emphasis on teachers being experts on the teaching of early reading? This all stems from the robust evidence which demonstrates that if children do not learn to read well and a child's early language acquisition is not secure, this can impact negatively on many aspects of that child's life. For example, research conducted by the Early Intervention Foundation (Law et al., 2017) outlines many of the negative consequences of poor language acquisition, which include:

- Those with early language difficulties are much more likely to struggle with reading as an adult.
- Children from disadvantaged backgrounds are more likely to have language difficulties.
- Links can be made between poor language acquisition and mental wellbeing.

Early reading forms one part of language development, as a lot is also developed through oracy and communication, but if we support all children to be able to read at the earliest possible opportunity, we are providing them with a real chance of having a successful education and being able to access the full curriculum.

As is referenced in the Teachers' Standards and the Core Content Framework, phonics is a key part of early reading and we will discuss the importance of phonics later, but, for now, early reading has many other components, including:

- engaging story times when adults share the best books with children
- teaching children nursery rhymes to learn and sing
- supporting adults at home to read with their children
- re-telling and role play of stories children are familiar with
- visiting the library and exposing children to a range of exciting texts
- having a classroom environment which supports a love of literature.

Research conducted by the Education Endowment Foundation (EEF) provides us with some guidance around what research-informed practice might look like. You can read its full recommendations on the EEF's website, but a summary of some of the early reading suggestions there include the following:

- There should be a balance between developing decoding and comprehension. Whilst decoding is extremely important, it is also critical that children develop comprehension skills.
- It is important for children to develop a love of reading and this will come through motivation.
- The phonics scheme used by the school must be comprehensive and implemented effectively (including staff training and the close monitoring of the impact on pupils).
- Specific strategies should be introduced which develop comprehension.
- There should be targeted additional support for those children who require it. (EEF, 2020)

Phonics

As mentioned above, both the Core Content Framework and the Teachers' Standards require those teaching early reading to understand how to teach phonics well. The Educational Endowment toolkit for teaching and learning notes that phonics is one of the most evidence-informed approaches we have in education, and that it can add +5 months to a child's learning, so it is an extremely important aspect of a child's education. In the UK, we have a statutory phonics assessment which is administered to all those in Year 1 (administered one to one with a familiar adult, where children read 40 words) to check children's word reading, and those who do not meet the threshold in Year 1 are assessed again in Year 2, emphasising the importance the government places on children learning to master phonics in KS1.

The EEF research advises that 'the teaching of phonics should be explicit and systematic to support children in making connections between the sound patterns they hear in words and the way that these words are written.' With this in mind, it is extremely important that we have a systematic programme of phonics in place for the children we teach, as when they develop early fluency in their reading, they are more likely to be successful readers as they progress through school.

All schools you work in will have a phonics teaching programme and this will be sequenced for you so that children progress in their phonics. This will support you in knowing what sounds the children should already know and what they should learn next. All phonics teaching will have started when children begin their reception year (some children will start in nursery). A key aspect of effective phonics teaching is that schools only use one phonics programme with fidelity and do not mix and match approaches, as the latter will increase the risk of children not building on prior learning and could create gaps in their phonemic awareness. In order to support schools to choose an effective systematic synthetic phonics teaching programme, the Department for Education (DfE) created criteria for a phonics programme to self-assess itself in order to be recognised as a DfE-validated programme. It is not a statutory requirement for schools to use a DfE-validated scheme, however it is highly likely your school will use one. At the time of writing this chapter (January 2023), there were 30 different validated programmes recommended by the DfE, so each school will use the programme it has chosen and it is important you are fully trained in how to teach, using the programme your school has selected.

The DfE describes a complete systematic synthetic phonics (SSP) programme as one that provides:

- all that is essential to teach SSP to children in the reception and Key Stage 1 years of mainstream primary school
- sufficient support for children in reception and Key Stage 1 to become fluent readers

- a structured route for most children to meet or exceed the expected standard in the Year 1 phonics screening check
- all National Curriculum expectations for word reading through decoding by the end of Key Stage 1.

You will find below some advice on what effective teaching in phonics should include, but here are some other tips for you to ensure phonics is secure within your classroom:

- Ensure you fully understand the phonics programme within your school. Observe teachers and have others observe you to provide feedback.
- Ensure your reading scheme aligns with your phonics scheme. Children should be reading books which provide them with the opportunity to practise the sounds they have learnt, and this will support fluency. It is OK for children to read the same book numerous times as the aim is to develop phonetic knowledge, so practice will support this. Such books are often referred to as decodable books.
- Ensure you closely follow the phonics approach of your school – sometimes this might seem a bit repetitive but the consistency of approach means children can focus on learning what you are teaching.
- Plan in time to revisit sounds you have taught the children, and if you ever find you have a spare 5 minutes, use this time to recap learning in phonics.
- Work with parents/carers to help them understand the phonics programme used by the school so they can support their child at home.

We have stressed the importance of children mastering phonics at the earliest opportunity and all children should have achieved this by the end of KS1 at the latest. We will have children in our class who may be slower to master phonics (they may have a special need, be new to English or just need a little more time) than others and it is extremely important that we put provision in place to ensure these children catch up with their peers. The DfE's reading framework (2022a) offers advice on how we might support these learners.

Teachers should:

- provide pupils with the skills and knowledge they need to read and spell, by direct instruction, progressing systematically with carefully structured, small and cumulative steps
- use instructional routines that become familiar
- provide materials that limit distraction; are clear, linear and easy to follow; are age-neutral or age-appropriate and can be adapted further, such as being reduced to individual items
- provide opportunities for work on vocabulary, fluency and reading comprehension
- provide multiple opportunities for overlearning (recall, retrieval, practice and application at the level of the alphabetic code, word, sentence and text). (DfE, 2022a: 56–57)

Teaching should:

- be at a suitable pace for the child because progression through a programme will be much slower than for their typically developing peers
- be daily, with well-paced, well-planned lessons that are engaging and motivating
- take full account of the child's individual strengths, weaknesses, knowledge and understanding, and profile of needs. (DfE, 2022a: 56–57)

Some children may need additional strategies such as those who:

- have physical disabilities that affect their fine motor control for holding and manipulating objects, e.g. the use of desktop manipulatives, alternative writing strategies
- are pre- or non-verbal, e.g. use of alternative communication strategies, such as selecting their response from auditory choices anchored to visual symbols or place-markers
- have both fine motor difficulties and are pre- or non-verbal, e.g. use of low- or high-tech eye-gaze strategies. (DfE, 2022a: 56–57)

Early Years

Early reading features strongly in the statutory framework for the Early Years Foundation Stage; there is a word reading early learning goal which outlines what children at the expected level of development will be able to do:

- say a sound for each letter in the alphabet and at least 10 digraphs
- read words consistent with their phonic knowledge by sound-blending
- read aloud simple sentences and books that are consistent with their phonics knowledge, including some common exception words. (DfE, 2021a: 13)

There is also a comprehension early learning goal which states that children with expected development will:

- demonstrate understanding of what has been read to them by retelling stories and narratives using their own words and recently introduced vocabulary
- anticipate – where appropriate – key events in stories
- use and understand recently introduced vocabulary during discussions about stories, non-fiction, rhymes and poems and during role play. (DfE, 2021a: 13)

Early years practitioners will often be extremely skilled at developing early language and reading, so it is always worth visiting the EYFS provision within your school to observe interactions and the language development opportunities, and to see how a love of reading is developed. You will notice how communication is encouraged for all children and you can speak to staff about what rhymes and stories the children know.

It is in reception year that daily phonics starts for most children (some may start in nursery), and the phonics approach used by a school will determine what the structure of these sessions looks like. We need to have the ambition that children will keep up with their phonics from the start and when we teach high-quality phonics we have a greater chance of achieving this. Phonics sessions may be brief at the start of the year, however as the year progresses, children should all be receiving high-quality phonics sessions which include direct input from the teacher and response from and application by the children. You will likely see opportunities within the EYFS environment for children to apply their phonetic knowledge, and those children who are not keeping up with their peers should be receiving opportunities for further phonics practice right from reception so they can keep up with their peers.

Elements of the Early Reading Curriculum

As mentioned above, a large part of the early reading children learning is experienced within the early years. However, the National Curriculum places a strong emphasis on children finishing Key Stage 1 as fluent readers who have a love of books. The design of the National Curriculum in Year 1 puts a strong emphasis on reading so that children have a good grasp of this before encountering more of the writing curriculum in Year 2.

Table 5.1 shows what children in KS1 should learn in word reading, according to the National Curriculum.

Table 5.2 provides a summary of what children in KS1 should learn in comprehension, according to the National Curriculum.

How Do You Build Subject Knowledge?

For most early career teachers who have not worked in a school before, the teaching of phonics will be new. It is essential that you develop a secure understanding of the principles which underpin teacher knowledge of phonics, and below is some advice on how you can achieve this.

Terminology: Your school will have a synthetic phonics programme which will outline how you should teach phonics to align with this approach, and this programme will support you in understanding what terminology to use when teaching as some programmes have vocabulary which is unique to their approach.

Table 5.1 National Curriculum – word reading

Year 1	Year 2
• apply phonic knowledge and skills as the route to decode words • respond speedily with the correct sound to **graphemes** (letters or groups of letters) for all 40+ **phonemes**, including, where applicable, alternative sounds for graphemes • read accurately by blending sounds in unfamiliar words containing GPCs that have been taught • read common exception words, noting unusual correspondences between spelling and sound and where these occur in the word • read words containing taught GPCs and -s, -es, -ing, -ed, -er and -est endings • read other words of more than one syllable that contain taught GPCs • read words with contractions (for example, I'm, I'll, we'll), and understand that the apostrophe represents the omitted letter(s) • read aloud accurately books that are consistent with their developing phonic knowledge and that do not require them to use other strategies to work out words • re-read these books to build up their fluency and confidence in word reading.	• continue to apply phonic knowledge and skills as the route to decode words until automatic decoding has become embedded and reading is fluent • read accurately by blending the sounds in words that contain the graphemes taught so far, especially recognising alternative sounds for graphemes • read accurately words of two or more syllables that contain the same graphemes as above • read words containing common suffixes, read further common exception words, noting unusual correspondences between spelling and sound and where these occur in the word • read most words quickly and accurately, without overt sounding and blending, when they have been frequently encountered • read aloud books closely matched to their improving phonic knowledge, sounding out unfamiliar words accurately, automatically and without undue hesitation • re-read these books to build up their fluency and confidence in word reading.

However, there is some generic terminology we all should know when teaching phonics:

- **Phoneme** is the word we use to describe the smallest unit of sound.
- **Grapheme** is the word we use to describe a group of different letters combining together to make a single phoneme.
- **The alphabetic code** refers to the correspondence between phonemes and the actual letters which represent these phonemes. In the English alphabet, we have 26 letters but roughly 44 sounds. In order to help teach these sounds, they have been organised into the alphabetic code and we teach children these sound/letter correspondences to help them read more successfully. At the end of the National Curriculum content for English, you can find a copy of the international phonetic alphabet which will support your understanding.

Table 5.2 National Curriculum – comprehension

Year 1	Year 2
Develop pleasure in reading, motivation to read, vocabulary and understanding by:	Develop pleasure in reading, motivation to read, vocabulary and understanding by:

Year 1:

- listening to and discussing a wide range of poems, stories and non-fiction at a level beyond that at which they can read independently
- being encouraged to link what they read or hear to their own experiences
- becoming very familiar with key stories, fairy stories and traditional tales, retelling them and considering their particular characteristics
- recognising and joining in with predictable phrases
- learning to appreciate rhymes and poems, and to recite some by heart
- discussing word meanings, linking new meanings to those already known

Understand both the books they can already read accurately and fluently and those they listen to by:

- drawing on what they already know or on background information and vocabulary provided by the teacher
- checking that the text makes sense to them as they read and correcting inaccurate reading
- discussing the significance of the title and events
- making inferences on the basis of what is being said and done
- predicting what might happen on the basis of what has been read so far

Participate in discussion about what is read to them, taking turns and listening to what others say
Explain clearly their understanding of what is read to them.

Year 2:

- listening to, discussing and expressing views about a wide range of contemporary and classic poetry, stories and non-fiction at a level beyond that at which they can read independently
- discussing the sequence of events in books and how items of information are related
- becoming increasingly familiar with and retelling a wider range of stories, fairy stories and traditional tales
- being introduced to non-fiction books that are structured in different ways
- recognising simple recurring literary language in stories and poetry
- discussing and clarifying the meanings of words, linking new meanings to known vocabulary
- discussing their favourite words and phrases
- continuing to build up a repertoire of poems learnt by heart, appreciating these and reciting some, with appropriate intonation to make the meaning clear

Understand both the books that they can already read accurately and fluently and those that they listen to by:

- drawing on what they already know or on background information and vocabulary provided by the teacher
- checking that the text makes sense to them as they read and correcting inaccurate reading
- making inferences on the basis of what is being said and done
- answering and asking questions
- predicting what might happen on the basis of what has been read so far

Participate in discussion about books, poems and other works that are read to them and those that they can read for themselves, taking turns and listening to what others say
Explain and discuss their understanding of books, poems and other material, both those that they listen to and those that they read for themselves.

Appendix 9 of the DfE's reading framework provides you with a useful glossary to explain much of the other terminology you will come across when learning how to teach phonics (common exception words, digraph, trigraph, etc.) and we would advise that you use this to develop your subject knowledge.

Synthetic phonics programme: As we touched on earlier, your school will have a phonics programme they follow. It is essential that you are well trained in it and have secure subject knowledge to teach the programme as it is intended. If your school is unable to offer direct training, there will be resources on the website of the phonics programme used by your school which will be able to support you to develop your knowledge of a particular programme. You should also make a request to observe some of the strongest teachers teaching phonics.

Literature knowledge: You can see from the KS1 content that there is an expectation that teachers instil a love of reading and share different stories and poems. This requires you to have knowledge of literature. The UKLA website (https://ukla.org) is a great resource to find a range of age-appropriate texts you can share with the children you teach; it also offers a wide range of diverse authors and characters.

When we consider pedagogical knowledge, we are considering how best to teach early reading. When we share stories with the children we teach, we must be engaging and inspire a love for the books we read.

Most synthetic phonics programmes will guide teachers with the pedagogical knowledge they need to have when teaching their phonics approach. However, the reading framework (DfE, 2022a) offers guidance around what strong pedagogical knowledge might look like:

- Be clear about the objectives for any session and make sure that the children understand them (e.g. 'By the end of this week, you will all be able to read these sounds; today we are learning the first one').
- Expect all children to participate throughout phonics sessions, for example by using 'call and response'.
- Make the most of the time for teaching and use activities that maximise the number of words children have to read and spell.
- Make sure that children practise using the knowledge they have been taught in previous lessons until they can use it automatically, thus freeing up their capacity to learn new knowledge.
- Support the children to connect the new knowledge with their previous learning.
- Demonstrate new learning in bite-sized chunks.
- Ensure children are given opportunities to apply what they have learnt.
- Praise the children for working hard and paying attention, being specific about what they have done well.
- Use assessment to determine the next steps clearly, including identifying those children who might need immediate extra support. (DfE, 2022a: 48)

Summary

What we have discussed in this chapter:

- Why it is important that we teach early reading well in primary school. If we support children to read well and not let a language gap grow, we are setting them up for a more successful education.
- That early reading includes a number of different components such as phonics, story times, sharing rhymes and songs.
- That your school will have a phonics programme it uses, and that it is essential you understand the dynamics of this programme so you can teach it as it is intended.
- The importance of catching any children who fall behind in phonics.
- Pupils having access to decodable books which support them to practise what they have learnt in phonics.
- How early reading is a key part of the EYFS framework, and that the DfE reading framework is really useful in developing your knowledge of early reading.
- That pupils in EYFS and KS1 learn both word reading and comprehension. The KS1 curriculum content has been mapped out so you can see the progression.
- The importance of building your subject knowledge and some strategies you can use to build your subject knowledge in early reading.
- A range of resources you can refer to.

Signposts to Additional Resources

There is an array of excellent resources to support the teaching of early reading but some resources we would recommend are outlined below:

- The Centre for Literacy in Primary Education has created reading scales to support the development of reading, and they can be found here: https://clpe. org.uk/teaching-resources/reading-and-writing-scales
- The Department for Education's reading framework provides guidance to support the effective teaching of reading (https://assets.publishing. service.gov.uk/government/uploads/system/uploads/attachment_data/ file/1102800/Reading_framework_teaching_the_foundations_of_literacy_-_ Sept_22.pdf)
- The Education Endowment Foundation has conducted a lot of research on early language, and its document (https://educationendowmentfoundation. org.uk/education-evidence/teaching-learning-toolkit/phonics) outlines its phonics research and recommendations.

- The Early Intervention Foundation paper (Law et al., 2017) referenced earlier can be read here: www.eif.org.uk/report/language-as-a-child-wellbeing-indicator
- Each region is supported by a government-funded 'English hub', whose primary focus is supporting the development of early reading. English hubs will have early reading experts who can support the development of reading – they offer free courses, consultancy, and can be a great resource to support early career teachers. If you visit the English Hubs website (www.englishhubs. org), you will be able to find your local hub and see what support it can offer.

QUESTIONS TO ASK EXPERTS

The Initial Teacher Training Core Content Framework (DfE, 2019a) specifies that during your training you need to have input from experts. Here are some early reading questions you could ask when you have the chance:

- What phonics scheme do we use? What is the rationale for this?
- What CPD is available to ensure everyone is teaching the phonics scheme consistently?
- How does the school catch up any children who fall behind in phonics?
- How is a love for reading developed?

Discussion Questions

1 In small groups, read the Early Learning Goals for word reading and comprehension. Which elements do you think are most important? Why?
2 In small groups, discuss what stories you know that you think it would be important to share with children and that would develop a love of reading. Why have you chosen these particular books?
3 How might you help a child who is not making enough progress in phonics?
4 How might you develop a love of reading in children?

6

ENGLISH

Why Teach English to Primary Children?

There are four elements to a primary English curriculum: speaking, listening, reading and writing. The golden thread running through all of these elements is communication. As humans, we are social, we talk to one another. We laugh, comfort, encourage, teach, and, with those same communication skills, we can argue, hurt and create conflict. Effective communication has the potential to avoid conflict – from the small disagreements in the playground to international friction that can lead to war. If we, as humans, can communicate effectively, we can negotiate, recognise our shared intentions and then cooperate and collaborate.

To communicate well, individuals need a voice. That voice may be expressed in various ways: through speaking, through writing stories, speeches, poetry, perhaps through other artistic expression. If there is one fundamental purpose of primary schooling, it is to help children find their voice.

An essential skill within communication is listening. In order to communicate effectively, we need to receive and interpret messages from others, both verbal and non-verbal. For primary children, their communication skills, both listening and speaking, develop within their play and their interactions with others. Before children are reading and writing, they will be speaking and listening, developing a vocabulary and building communication skills. As teachers, we can model effective communication, explicitly teach vocabulary and provide frequent opportunities for children to develop their communications skills.

The teaching of reading, as we explored in Chapter 5, unlocks the entire curriculum for primary children. Through systematic phonics teaching, we give children the tools they need to crack the code of reading. Once children can read fluently, they can read about the Ancient Egyptians, earthquakes, deep-sea creatures, and musicians – the world is suddenly accessible. When children are able to read, they can discover what sort of books they enjoy, and read for the pure pleasure they gain. The research around reading for pleasure has been collated in the report 'Research evidence on reading for pleasure' (DfE, 2012). Whilst reading for pleasure, children build background knowledge and vocabulary, develop their imagination and learn more about the world around them. Over time, children who read successfully can move from learning to read, to reading to learn.

Whilst children are developing spoken language, they will start to lay the foundations for developing writing skills. Writing starts before children begin to form letters. When a baby begins to reach for objects and grips with their hands, when they begin to crawl, when they take a stick and bang it against the floor, they are developing the strength in their upper body, arms and hands that is essential for later writing skills. In the early years, when a young child kneads playdough, uses tweezers to pick up small beads, weaves a ribbon to make a basket, or makes marks using a paintbrush and paint, they are further developing the muscle strength and coordination needed for later writing skills.

Within the primary curriculum, children are taught to form the letters needed to write words. They are then taught to compose writing based on their own ideas, speaking a sentence aloud before writing it. They are taught to read their writing to check if it makes sense. Spelling, punctuation and grammar are taught throughout the primary curriculum, supporting children to make choices in their writing for accuracy or for developing different writing styles.

How Is English Subject Knowledge Sequenced?

The National Curriculum document of all the subjects combined is nearly 200 pages in length, however the English part of this document is 80 pages, demonstrating the importance we place on this subject in primary school.

You can read more information about the content of the English curriculum below, however one of the reasons that this subject is so long is that it includes some really useful appendices which sequence some of the curriculum aspects (spellings, grammar, vocabulary and punctuation) for us in a year-by-year manner, making it clear to see what we should teach and in what year group. This also helps us to look back on what children should have learnt previously so we can build on this knowledge.

The curriculum content in English for KS1 is set out year by year so it makes it clear to us what children should learn each year, and in KS2 it is set out in lower KS2 (Years 3 and 4) and upper KS2 (Years 5 and 6), which again makes it easier for us to track how content is sequenced across key stages.

When it comes to sequencing English, the greater challenge is how we break down the year group content into small steps so that children can meet the end-of-year expectations.

Let's explore how we would sequence a Key Stage 2 unit of work in English. If we look at the expectations for the end of KS2 in composition, we can see that children should be able to plan, draft, write, evaluate and edit their writing.

What Do I Want My Children to Know and Be Able to Do at the End of This Unit?

Let's imagine we are planning for a Year 6 class – by the end of this unit, I want children to have a completed piece of writing which they have planned well, drafted and improved, edited and which they can evaluate the effectiveness of. I will need to decide the context the children will write within. For the purpose of this example, I want my children to be able to write a persuasive letter to the school headteacher to convince them to allow the children to go on a school trip of their choosing.

Where Will I Start?

When we embark upon planning a sequenced unit of work in English, as with other curriculum areas, we need to reconnect children to their previous learning.

You may want to ask yourself the following:

- What have the children already studied in previous years? How can I connect this new learning to the previous learning? What vocabulary have they been taught before? Which punctuation and grammar tools have they learned so far? Have they written persuasively before? How can I deliberately connect this?

- I know the content for Years 3 and 4 requires children to plan, draft and evaluate their writing, so I want to understand what existing knowledge they have around these aspects so I can build on their learning. Are there examples of previous writing I can see?
- What can I do to support those children who may need more help with aspects of English? For example, would some children benefit from a scaffold such as a word bank to support their spellings? Do I need to consider a specific planning template for these children?

We then need to consider our sequence of learning: what do I want pupils to know? What genre will we be writing in? How will I help them understand the impact they want to achieve? Which words or grammar devices do I want them to use confidently and how will I connect this to the genre? Will I use any texts to support their understanding? How will I check children understand what I intended them to learn? How will I teach planning, evaluating and drafting? What is my end goal for this unit?

What Will My Sequence of Learning Look Like?

A sequence of learning in English will not always look exactly the same as another, but here is an example structure:

Step 1: I would set the scene for the children. I would share the end point of writing a persuasive letter and set an engaging context (school trip). I would begin by sharing examples of when they have previously written persuasively and recap some of their learning from this. Following this, I would share an example of a good persuasive letter and discuss the impact of this letter (persuading the headteacher to let them go on a trip). I would teach the children the persuasive devices used to achieve the persuasive impact (I would explicitly identify those features they should be familiar with) and discuss which of these we could use in our writing effectively. I would share more examples of persuasive writing for the children to analyse, with a focus on what makes them strong persuasive pieces of writing. By the end of this step, I would want the children to know what a good persuasive letter looks like and why. By showing them a number of examples, the children will understand that there isn't one precise way to write this. I will also show the children some poor examples of persuasive letters so they can see when the impact has not been achieved, and I will plan for these to include some misconceptions.

Step 2: I would directly teach children the grammar and punctuation they could use to make their letters persuasive. I would use appendix 2 of the National Curriculum and look at the content for Year 6. For example, I can see children need to be taught a range of cohesive devices and this would suit this genre well to help the writing flow. I would reconnect with their Year 5 learning on building cohesion within a paragraph and check their understanding. Once I am satisfied they understand this, I would introduce them to a wider range of cohesive devices which they can use to support their persuasive letter (e.g. the use of adverbials or repetition of a phrase or word). I would model examples and provide children with the opportunity to deliberately practise using cohesive devices to build fluency and understanding. I would also show poor examples to tackle misconceptions.

Step 3: I would teach the children how to plan for their writing effectively. I would connect with their previous planning experiences. I would model this on the board for the children to see how I am modelling my plan (I may use a template for this) and I would deliberately teach aspects of planning (versus writing at length). I would think aloud, making clear connections with the grammar knowledge and persuasive devices already taught. I would also model editing and improving my plan. As well as modelling my planning, I would eventually ask the children to help with my planning and gather their ideas so I can check their understanding. The children would then plan their writing. I would ensure all children have enough time to plan well, especially those who have English as an additional language or a special need, and I would ensure I have an appropriate planning system for them. Planning may take a number of lessons and my planning would include vocabulary, phrases, grammar, and so on, and I would want the children to consider carefully how they will use their plan in their writing, and encourage my strongest writers to bring their own ideas. As children are planning, I will provide in-the-moment feedback.

Step 4: I would now model writing for the children so they can see how I am turning my plan into extended writing. I will think aloud and also model making some changes so children know they do not have to stick rigidly to their plan. I will constantly refer back to the impact and stop and consider if I think this will persuade the headteacher by reading my writing back and reflecting upon whether it is persuasive. After some modelling, I will bring the children's ideas in to check for their understanding. The children will then write their own letter, with regular feedback (this may take place over a number of lessons).

Step 5: As the children complete some writing, I will model to the children how to proofread and edit. I will use my own written example for the children to see how I have evaluated and improved my writing. I will provide specific prompts to act as scaffolds to support the children to edit (again linking this to what they have learnt previously), and with any change I make, I will discuss how it makes my writing have a better impact. The children will then edit and improve their own writing.

Step 6: The children will write a final draft with all improvements made and send these to the headteacher. I will also provide children with time to evaluate their writing (I will model evaluating mine) so that they can reflect upon whether their writing was effective and how they might improve next time.

*Each step may be one or more lessons, depending on term length and timetabling.

What Does Progress Look Like Within This Unit?

Communication and Language is one of the three prime areas of learning in the early years, the other two being physical development and personal, social and emotional development. These areas are described in the EYFS framework as being vital for 'igniting children's curiosity and enthusiasm for learning, forming relationships and thriving' (DfE, 2021a). At the end of reception, children will be assessed against Early Learning Goals that break this area down into 'listening, attention and understanding' and 'speaking'. Early years teachers will make a judgement about children's development and will consider how children listen and interpret what they hear, how they ask questions, how they converse with their peers, how they offer ideas, how they use vocabulary, and how they express their ideas and feelings.

Literacy is one of the specific areas of learning within early years. The specific areas build on the prime areas of learning. If children are building strong foundations for communication and language, then literacy learning can flourish. Literacy in the early years refers to language comprehension, word reading and writing. In nursery and reception, children will be sharing books and be read to by adults, they will be learning rhymes, poems and songs, and they will retell stories orally in their own words, using puppets or props. They will begin to learn the grapheme/phoneme correspondence that is the foundation for phonic knowledge, and how to write the sounds they've learned before putting those sounds together to make words. You can see the Early Learning Goals for word reading and comprehension in Chapter 5.

Children in the early years will also be setting their foundation for writing. Children will learn letter formation and understand that print has meaning. Children will start with initial mark making, using a range of tools, and as they develop in the early years, they will begin writing simple phrases and sentences. The Early Learning Goal for writing will provide you with an indication of what children at the expected level of writing will be able to do:

- write recognisable letters, most of which are correctly formed
- spell words by identifying sounds in them and representing the sounds with a letter or letters
- write simple phrases and sentences that can be read by others. (DfE, 2021a)

It is worth noting that within the EYFS framework, aspects of handwriting such as pencil grip are found in the physical development content of the EYFS curriculum and not in Literacy as these aspects of a child's development relate more to their physical development at that age.

Key Elements of the English Curriculum

The key elements of the English curriculum at primary level are:

- spoken language
- reading
- writing
- spelling, punctuation and grammar.

The **programmes of study** for English are the largest of all subjects in the primary curriculum. A unique element to the English curriculum is that it sets out, year by year, what children should learn in reading and writing in Years 1 and 2, which makes it easier for KS1 teachers to know what children should know each year. In KS2, it combines expectations for Years 3 and 4 and for Years 5 and 6, so teachers know what children should be able to do by the end of Years 4 and 6. It will be up to the school to sequence the content into year groups for Years 3 and 5.

Spoken language

Spoken language is important for children's communication and for their learning across the curriculum. Children can come to school with very different experiences of spoken language, as cited in research by Hart and Risley (2003).

Some children will have a word-rich early experience, coming from homes with lots of talk and many books. Other children will not be so fortunate and will have heard fewer words, spoken fewer words and shared fewer books with an adult. As teachers, we must be attuned to children's spoken language level. We must create language-rich environments in our classroom, explicitly teaching vocabulary and modeling high-quality spoken language across the curriculum.

Throughout the curriculum, children must be taught how to listen and respond to others, how to voice their own thoughts and opinions, how to debate and discuss, and how to disagree. A good grasp of spoken language helps children to understand what they read and supports the formation of ideas for writing. Drama has an important role to play within the English curriculum and children should have opportunities to explore dramatic techniques, including improvisation, acting in roles, reading and writing scripts and performing to a range of audiences.

Children must also have opportunities to respond to drama performances that they watch themselves.

The National Curriculum itself only dedicates one page to spoken English: it comprises of 12 bullet points which schools must cover in their curriculum from Years 1 to 6. It will be up to schools to sequence this learning across their curriculum.

Reading

Reading within the primary curriculum has two elements: word recognition and comprehension. In order to recognise words, children must be taught strategies to decode unfamiliar words and to recognise familiar words. In the early stages of reading, phonics teaches children what sound a letter, or a group of letters, makes. As we explored in Chapter 5, a single sound is called a phoneme and the letter or letters that make that sound is called a grapheme (e.g. 'a' or 'igh'). Knowing the link between the sound and the letter(s) is called grapheme-phoneme correspondence. Beginner readers can then approach an unfamiliar word by saying the sounds that make the word and blending those sounds together to read the word. As their phonic knowledge increases, they will be able to attempt more complex words. Over time, fluency increases as children learn and remember more sounds and become more confident, experienced readers.

Every school will have an approach to teaching children to read, and most schools will use a phonics programme. If you are new to a school, whatever year group you are in, it is important to understand how children are taught to read at that school. You may have children in upper KS2 that need further phonics instruction to help them read successfully, and it is important that your teaching is consistent with the approaches used within the school.

The National Curriculum for Years 1 and 2 has a strong emphasis on word reading, stressing the importance of children learning phonics at the earliest opportunity. We notice that word reading almost disappears from KS2 as the curriculum for the start of KS2 states: 'Most pupils will not need further direct teaching of word reading skills', however it does also recognise:

> Pupils who are still struggling to decode need to be taught to do this urgently through a rigorous and systematic phonics programme so that they catch up rapidly with their peers. If they cannot decode independently and fluently, they will find it increasingly difficult to understand what they read and to write down what they want to say.

Alongside word recognition and the skill of decoding, children are developing comprehension, understanding what they read. It is possible for children to become very skilled at decoding so that it appears they can 'read' anything. However, what must sit alongside the decoding skills is an understanding of the content they are reading. Comprehension is not a skill that can be taught in isolation; it draws on a wide vocabulary and knowledge of the world.

An example of the importance of comprehension would be a child reading about an environmental disaster after an oil spill in a non-fiction text. In order to fully understand this, a child would need knowledge of oceans, countries and continents, shipping, oil and fuels, sea currents and sea creatures. They would need geography knowledge and science knowledge alongside their knowledge of the sounds that make the words they are reading. A child could read the words in a book if they had been taught the required phonemes, but they may not have secured the necessary background knowledge (Hirsch, 2006). In Key Stages 1 and 2, the foundation subjects, for example history, geography, science and art, have a really important role to play in reading comprehension. The content of these subjects helps children to gain knowledge of the world, which they can use to understand what they are reading. Understanding supports confidence growth and encourages children to read more and widely.

Curriculum content for comprehension features in all year groups and, as mentioned earlier, the KS2 curriculum for reading is very much focused on comprehension as there is an expectation that children's working memory can now focus on meaning as they will be fluent readers. By the end of Year 2, the National Curriculum states that pupils should be taught to do the following as part of comprehension:

- develop pleasure in reading, motivation to read, vocabulary and understanding
- understand both the books that they can already read accurately and fluently and those that they listen to
- participate in discussion about books, poems and other works that are read to them and those that they can read for themselves, taking turns and listening to what others say
- explain and discuss their understanding of books, poems and other material, both those that they listen to and those that they read for themselves.

The above sets the standard for what children should be able to do by the end of KS1 and it is important you read the content for the year group you teach as well as the year before so that you know what children should be able to do. By the end of Year 4, children should:

- have developed a positive attitude to reading and to understanding what they read
- be able to understand what they read, in books they can read independently
- be adept at retrieving and recording information from non-fiction
- be able to participate in discussion both about books that are read to them and those they can read for themselves, taking turns and listening to what others say.

By end of Year 6, children should be able to:

- maintain a positive attitude to reading and to understanding what they read
- understand what they read
- discuss and evaluate how authors use language, including figurative language, considering the impact on the reader
- distinguish between statements of fact and opinion
- retrieve, record and present information from non-fiction
- participate in discussions about books that are read to them and those they can read for themselves, building on their own and others' ideas and challenging views courteously
- explain and discuss their understanding of what they have read, including through formal presentations and debates, maintaining a focus on the topic and using notes where necessary
- provide reasoned justifications for their views.

The curriculum includes further content on how you might teach the above, and some elements are broken down into further bullet points, which is why it is important that you read the full year group content for the year you teach.

Writing

Within the English curriculum, writing has two important elements: transcription and composition. Transcription includes spelling and handwriting; it is the act of writing words on a page. Composition focuses on gathering ideas in a coherent manner and structuring these ideas into sentences for writing. Children must learn that editing and revising are part of a writing process, that writers don't create a perfect piece of writing at the first attempt; rather, they draft and redraft until they are happy with their creation.

Many schools use a programme for developing handwriting and may have a specific approach to cursive or 'joined up' handwriting. It is important to familiarise yourself with the handwriting approach within a school and to practise any formations you must model within your lessons. Supporting children to form legible writing in a fluent manner will help them to write down their ideas and grow in confidence as writers. The sooner children can form letters fluently, the more space they will have in their working memory to focus on the content of their writing.

When children begin to think about the structure of writing, they need to think about their ideas and how they organise them into a coherent structure. Children will be taught to think about the purpose of their writing and who the audience is. Children's knowledge of vocabulary will translate into writing as they select words for clarity or for effect. If children are reading widely and being explicitly taught vocabulary across the curriculum, this will contribute to their composition within writing.

When considering the composition aspects of writing, it is interesting to note that the National Curriculum does not specifically outline what genres of writing children should learn. It is up to individual schools to decide what children will write about and in what context. This provides schools with a lot of freedom to engage with children's interests and you should ask your own school how they have planned writing units. The curriculum does outline some of the structures and processes you should teach children when they are composing writing, and by the end of KS2 children should be able to plan, draft, write, edit and evaluate their own writing.

Spelling, punctuation and grammar

There is statutory content for spelling, vocabulary, grammar and punctuation listed in the English National Curriculum. This content supports teachers to develop children's vocabulary and their understanding of how the English language is structured.

The appendices at the back of the English National Curriculum are the most useful documents to support you in understanding the curriculum requirements for spelling, vocabulary, grammar and punctuation.

Appendix 1: Spelling

The first appendix at the back of the curriculum focuses on spelling. For each year group, it outlines the statutory requirements, gives guidance for teaching the spelling and provides example words. This is useful for ensuring your subject knowledge is secure. The appendix also includes the statutory word lists for KS2 which pupils must learn. You should familiarise yourself with this for the year group you teach.

Appendix 2: Vocabulary, grammar and punctuation

Appendix 2 of the National Curriculum outlines exactly what children should be learning in each year group when it comes to vocabulary, grammar and punctuation. Each year group has a table which clearly outlines the word, sentence, text, punctuation and terminology for pupils. As this is already sequenced for us, we can see what the expectations are for each year group and the table provides us with real clarity around what we should be teaching and in what year group.

How Do You Build Subject Knowledge?

In each of the areas covered by the National Curriculum in English, we must have the specialised *content knowledge* required to teach the subject well. We also need *pedagogical knowledge*: knowledge of how to teach English in our primary classrooms.

We will all have different starting points with our subject knowledge in English and the subject knowledge audit in the appendix is always a useful starting point. Below are some suggestions for how you might build your own subject knowledge:

- Terminology: The English curriculum is full of technical terminology which we need to understand the meaning of and be able to explain. From antonyms to determiners to relative clauses, we need to be able to understand and explain these words to the children we teach. The best way to build your subject knowledge for these terms is the glossary within the English curriculum (at the end). This glossary outlines all the grammatical terms used within the English curriculum and will provide you with clear explanations and examples to support your subject knowledge.
- Handwriting: In a digital world, it might be hard to remember the last time you wrote at length using a pen or pencil! However, there are benefits to teaching children how to transcribe effectively and we need to be an expert in teaching this. As a teacher, you need to model clear handwriting as well as be able to teach it. There is no agreed handwriting format so your school will have decided which scheme/approach they wish to use and you should check this out with your school. Once you are aware of this, you should practise the formation of letters as and when you can. It is also important to familiarise yourself with how the scheme suggests the letter is formed – for example, it might suggest starting on the line, which you will need to model when forming this letter.
- Literature knowledge: In order to inspire a love of reading and writing, we need to know great texts to be able to read and share with our children. The Centre for Literacy in Primary Education (CLPE) provides a range of resources you can use to develop your knowledge of literature – the Centre provides a number of book lists which include a diverse range of authors and poets.
- Pedagogical knowledge: This refers to the knowledge we have around how we teach the different elements of the English curriculum. There is much to know about how to teach English well, however a useful starting point is the Educational Endowment Foundation (EEF) research on improving literacy. The EEF has produced some useful recommendations for the teaching of literacy (they use this phrase instead of English) in KS1 and KS2, which will support you in understanding what research-informed choices you can make around how to teach English. The research outlines language, reading and writing

advice for you to consider. You can find the research for KS1 and KS2 at the following links:

- ○ KS1: https://educationendowmentfoundation.org.uk/education-evidence/ guidance-reports/literacy-ks-1
- ○ KS2: https://educationendowmentfoundation.org.uk/education-evidence/ guidance-reports/literacy-ks2

Summary

What we have discussed in this chapter:

- What primary English prepares children for.
- That a high-quality English curriculum is well sequenced and clearly identifies what the children will learn from EYFS to Key Stage 2. This clarity helps teachers to teach effective lessons and helps children to learn, remember and be able to do more over time.
- That our own knowledge of both English subject content (what we teach) and **pedagogy** (how we teach) is crucial and will develop throughout our teaching career.

Signposts to Additional Resources

Exploring these resources will deepen your understanding of the role of English in the primary curriculum:

- The CLPE website has an array of resources to support you with your teaching of English. A particular resource we would recommend is the reading and writing scales the organisation has produced, that will help you develop your own understanding of how reading and writing might progress for a child – https://clpe.org.uk/research/reading-and-writing-scales
- The EEF website will provide you with a number of research-informed approaches to the teaching of English. In particular, read the guidance reports on the teaching of literacy – https://educationendowmentfoundation.org.uk/ education-evidence/guidance-reports
- The DfE's reading framework (2022a) will provide you with advice on how to lay the foundations in reading, and will offer clear guidance and reflection criteria to reflect upon.
- Ofsted has produced an English research paper as part of its subject reviews which has recommendations for reading, writing and spoken English – www.gov.uk/ government/publications/curriculum-research-review-series-english/ curriculum-research-review-series-english

QUESTIONS TO ASK EXPERTS

The Initial Teacher Training Core Content Framework (DfE, 2019a) specifies that during your training you need to have input from experts. Here are some English education curriculum questions you could ask when you have the chance:

- Can you help me to understand how the English curriculum is structured?
- What materials are available to help me prepare my lessons?
- How are writing genres taught to children? Why did you choose these genres?
- What resources can I use to improve my own subject knowledge?
- What handwriting scheme do you use? What advice would you offer when teaching handwriting?
- What do we expect children in the year I am working in to be able to do in English?

Discussion Questions

- In small groups, read the Early Learning Goals for 'Communication and Language' and 'Literacy'. Discuss the importance of vocabulary in unlocking the world of English.
- In small groups, read the National Curriculum statutory content for spoken English. How do knowledge and skills build over time?
- How can we help develop reading for pleasure in our classrooms?
- Which areas of English do you want to learn more about to secure your subject knowledge? How will you do this, and what resources will you use?

7

MATHS

Why Do We Teach Mathematics?

'Everything is maths and physics.' (Katherine Johnson, NASA STEM Conference, Cape Canaveral, Florida, 2010)

Mathematics is one of the primary core subjects, taking up over 40 pages of the National Curriculum document. It is also one of the few subjects which is statutory across all the primary key stages. So, why is this subject so important?

There are many reasons why we teach maths, three important ones being as follows:

- Numbers are at the heart of daily living: from telling the time to paying for goods to managing banking. Without a strong understanding in maths, day-to-day living will be more challenging.

- Maths is a gateway into many other disciplines, such as physics, engineering, economics, history and music.
- Many future professions and university courses require a certain level of maths to even be considered. Not ensuring our children have a strong foundation in maths may hinder them from future opportunity.

It is not uncommon for people to say, 'I'm just not good at maths' or 'I don't have a maths brain', but, as primary teachers, it is our job to ensure *all* of our children master the primary curriculum before they enter Key Stage 3. As primary pupils work through the primary curriculum, they will become more confident in mastering its three aims – fluency, reasoning and problem solving:

1   Become fluent in the fundamentals of mathematics, including through varied and frequent practice with increasingly complex problems over time, so that pupils develop conceptual understanding and the ability to recall and apply knowledge rapidly and accurately.
2   Reason mathematically by following a line of enquiry, conjecturing relationships and generalisations, and developing an argument, justification or proof, using mathematical language
3   Solve problems by applying their mathematics to a variety of routine and non-routine problems with increasing sophistication, including breaking down problems into a series of simpler steps and persevering in seeking solutions. (DfE, 2013a: 12)

As trainee teachers, we need to be able to deliver the curriculum in a way that enables our pupils to develop and consolidate their understanding of the three aims above, and we need to think carefully about our use of resources and lesson design.

Ofsted (2021a) published a review into mathematics. The review explored research from Ofsted inspections and wider literature around mathematics; it concluded that pupils in England tend to perform better than their counterparts in other countries, however it noted that disadvantaged children are much less likely to meet the expected standard at the end of EYFS, Key Stage 1 and Key Stage 2.

The Ofsted research review in mathematics (2021a) found the following which are important for teaching to consider:

- Teachers must close the entry gap in knowledge relating to facts, vocabulary, symbols and concepts.
- The teaching of facts should be sequenced so it helps pupils to learn methods (we will explore sequencing further).
- Teaching should be clear and systematic.
- We should aim for pupils to become proficient as this develops motivation and confidence.
- Pupils need regular opportunities to rehearse what they have learnt.

- Assessment should focus on component knowledge (assessing what has been taught) as this is more useful for gap analysis.
- Written work should be systematic and orderly as this supports pupils in avoiding errors and seeing connections.

Additionally, research from the Educational Endowment (EEF) provides primary teachers with useful recommendations for improving mathematics. What is especially useful about how the organisation has conducted its research is that it has provided specific recommendations for the early years (EYFS) and Key Stage 1 (KS1) (EEF, 2021) and separate recommendations for Key Stage 2 (KS2) (EEF, 2022).

The organisation's EYFS and KS1 research (EEF, 2021) suggests five key recommendations:

1   Ensure teachers have a secure understanding of how children learn maths.
2   Provide wider opportunities for pupils to apply maths throughout the day.
3   Make use of manipulatives and images to support understanding.
4   Ensure new learning builds on existing knowledge.
5   Ensure additional support is of a high quality.

Its research for KS2 (EEF, 2022) suggests eight key recommendations:

1   Make effective use of assessment.
2   As above, use manipulatives and images to support teaching.
3   Specifically teach children how to problem-solve.
4   Support pupils to make connections in their mathematical knowledge.
5   Support pupils to be motivated and independent in maths.
6   Ensure the resources used and tasks set support learning meaningfully.
7   Ensure that additional support/interventions are of a high quality.
8   Ensure procedures for pupils transitioning from Year 6 to 7 are meaningful.

You will notice that some of the research from both Ofsted and the EEF align, which supports primary teachers to be strategic in selecting appropriate, research-informed strategies to support our teaching of maths. It goes without saying that the above is a top-level view of a much bigger piece of research which we highly recommend you read in more detail (links are provided at the end of the chapter).

How Is Maths Subject Knowledge Sequenced?

The national curriculum for maths sets out what should be taught, year by year, and this makes sequencing the curriculum much easier. This curriculum builds on what the children will have learnt in early years as part of the statutory framework for the Early Years Foundation Stage (DfE, 2021a). Whilst the EYFS framework is not structured year by year, it outlines what children should have achieved before they enter Year 1, for example children should understand the number 10 (we will discuss maths in the EYFS later in this chapter).

When considering the maths curriculum for Key Stages 1 and 2, you can see from Table 7.1 that number, measurement and geometry are taught in each year group, but some topics are not encountered until the children are older.

Under each of these macro topics, the curriculum breaks down what children should learn in each year. This means that children can learn each aspect in a sequential way and this knowledge will be built upon when children encounter the topic again.

Let's look at an example: If we take a top-level view, you can see that the number strand has numerous components – number and place value; addition and subtraction; multiplication and division and fractions. If we just look at one strand of fractions and we explore the concept of equivalency, we will be able to look at how knowledge builds year by year. In Year 1, children are taught about half and quarter, but in Year 2 they come across equivalency for the first time.

You can see how children mastering knowledge in a previous year will mean they can sequentially build on what they learnt previously and use existing knowledge to help understand new curriculum content.

Whilst the above provides a useful overview of how the entire maths curriculum is sequenced, it is our job to consider the smaller building blocks of knowledge within each year group so we can ensure our pupils learn what is expected by the end of that year.

Let us now look at a specific example for Key Stage 2, Year 3: pupils are taught equivalent fractions with small denominators – let's consider how we would sequence this.

What Do I Want my Children to Know and be Able to Do at the End of this Unit?

By the end of Year 3, children should be taught equivalent fractions with small denominators. I need to decide what small denominators and equivalences I want the children to know by the time they are finished learning this unit. I decide I want them to know equivalent fractions with denominators up to 10.

Table 7.1 Overview of topics taught in the KS1 and KS2 maths curriculum

Year 1	Number	Measurement	Geometry			
Year 1	Number	Measurement	Geometry			
Year 2	Number	Measurement	Geometry	Statistics		
Year 3	Number	Measurement	Geometry	Statistics		
Year 4	Number	Measurement	Geometry	Statistics		
Year 5	Number	Measurement	Geometry	Statistics		
Year 6	Number	Measurement	Geometry	Statistics	Ratio and Proportion	Algebra

Where will I Start?

I will think about what they may already know about equivalent fractions. I will find out what they have learnt previously in their maths curriculum, and I will check they have remembered this information. I can review any assessment information I have and I will also look at the Year 2 maths curriculum. I can see in Year 2 that they are taught the equivalence of ½ and ¾ so this is a good starting point for me. I will ask questions and plan tasks to check the children have retained this knowledge and I will also consider targeted support for any children who have not retained this or who are new to my class, and ensure this is in place to close the knowledge gap.

What will my Sequence of Learning Look Like?

I will break the new knowledge down into building blocks, so I am introducing it in small, manageable chunks. My sequence of learning may look like this*:

Step 1: Reconnect with prior learning, reminding the children what equivalent means and linking this to examples they will be familiar with.

Step 2: Using concrete resources such as Cuisenaire rods, I will introduce wider equivalent fractions so the children can see, in a concrete manner, how different fractions are equivalent. I may also use strips of paper and fraction walls to support the children to see how different fractions can be equivalent.

Step 3: As children develop their understanding, I will link their new knowledge of equivalent fractions with number lines between 0 and 1. I will teach them how they can use these number lines to find equivalent fractions.
I will still allow some children who need the Cuisenaire rods/strips of paper to use these to scaffold their learning but, for the majority, I will guide them towards only using a number line. As I am not going above denominators of 10, I will not go above this number when dividing my number line.

Step 4: Once children have had enough practice, I will teach them how to reason and problem-solve so they can apply their knowledge – for example, we may link some of the visuals I used previously with equivalent fractions, or I will get the children to problem-solve with fractions that have missing numerators or denominators so they can find equivalent fractions. If some children have not yet achieved the previous step, I may choose to give them more practice before they try reasoning and problem solving (but I will ensure they do get some experience of those).

*Each step may be taught in one lesson or more than one.

What Does Progress Look Like Within this Unit?

When we consider progress in this unit, we really want to see that children are developing their understanding of equivalency within the context of fractions. We expect to see children with a deep understanding that two fractions can numerically look different but, in fact, equal the same amount. We would also hope to see progress in the sense that children are becoming less reliant on concrete resources to recognise equivalent fractions and are using other strategies such as a number line. It is important I provide opportunities to re-visit this learning and when I do future assessments, they will be useful in telling me whether the children have remembered this over time.

In the examples above, we have looked at how the concept of equivalency is developed across the entire curriculum as well as how this can be broken down into smaller steps for each year group. The example provided was for a Key Stage 2 class.

Below is an example of how we might sequence another area of the curriculum into small steps, but this time the example is from Key Stage 1.

In Year 2, children need to be able to identify and describe the properties of 2D shapes, including the number of sides, and the line of symmetry in a vertical line. If you need to teach this aspect of the curriculum, you could use the same questions to support you to sequence lessons.

What Do I want my Children to be able to know and Do at the End of this Sequence of Lesson?

I want my children to be able to describe the properties of 2D shapes by the end of this unit. This will mean the children are able to tell me the number of sides and also how many lines of symmetry a shape has. I will plan some assessment questions now that I can use towards the end of the sequence of lessons which will check they have achieved what I want them to achieve.

What Do the Children Already Know that Might Help Them?

I know from the Year 1 curriculum that children should be able to recognise and name some common 2D shapes, so I will revisit this to confirm they know this and use this foundational knowledge to plan our next steps.

What will my Sequence of Learning Look Like?

I will break down the knowledge into small, manageable chunks and my sequence of learning might look like this over a series of lessons (note that more than one step might be covered in one lesson):

Step 1: I will reconnect with prior learning and remind the children what they learnt about 2D shapes in Year 1. We will revisit the names of some common 2D shapes and have concrete resources to check the children can all name the shapes. If any of them are unable to recall the names, they will have some focused teaching.

Step 2: I will tell the children that we will be learning about the properties of shapes. I will explain what properties are and ensure the children understand what this mathematical word means in relation to shape.

Step 3: I will link the new learning of properties with the existing knowledge of 2D shapes. I will model and teach number of lines for common shapes and focus on recognising the number of lines for common 2D shapes. The children will practise this with common 2D shapes and may begin to move from concrete to pictorial.

Step 4: I will now introduce the term symmetry as new learning and link this with the existing knowledge of properties and 2D shapes. I will teach children the new mathematical language and model to the children how to find a line of symmetry. I will provide concrete examples for the children to practise.

Step 5: I will begin to expect the children to reason and problem-solve, and shift my lessons to using more pictorial resources (with concrete still available for those who need it). This might take place over more than one lesson.

What Does Progress Look Like Within this Unit?

I will see progress through the children's use of mathematical language – can they use the word property correctly? Can they explain symmetry and provide examples?

Children should have progressed from knowing the names of common 2D shapes to now being able to describe properties and lines of symmetry. I should also see progress as children no longer require concrete resources to demonstrate their knowledge.

Early Years

When teaching Year 1, it is important to consider what children learn in the early years so you can build on this knowledge. Therefore, you could consider what the early learning goals (ELGs) expect children to achieve at the end of the reception year so you can build on this in Year 1.

Mathematics Number ELG

Children at the expected level of development will:

- have a deep understanding of number to 10, including the composition of each number
- subitise (recognise quantities without counting) up to 5
- automatically recall (without reference to rhymes, counting or other aids) number bonds up to 5 (including subtraction facts) and some number bonds to 10, including double facts. (DfE, 2022b)

Numerical Patterns ELG

Children at the expected level of development will:

- verbally count beyond 20, recognising the pattern of the counting system
- compare quantities up to 10 in different contexts, recognising when one quantity is greater than, less than or the same as the other quantity
- explore and represent patterns within numbers up to 10, including evens and odds, double facts, and how quantities can be distributed equally. (DfE, 2022b)

Whilst the early learning goals will provide teachers with a good indicator of what children have achieved by the end of the EYFS, it is important to note that these do not form a curriculum, and the maths curriculum experienced by children will go beyond the ELGs. For example, as part of the statutory framework for mathematics in the EYFS, children will learn about shape and measure but these are not included within the ELG statements.

Key Elements of the Maths Curriculum

We have already discussed many of the key elements of the maths curriculum, particularly as mentioned at the start of this chapter. The maths curriculum has three core aims, around fluency, reasoning and problem solving. You will see in the examples of sequencing above that we have planned for the children to become more fluent and to problem-solve and reason. These three aims are at the heart of the maths curriculum, however, as teachers, we need to also be aware of other key elements of the primary maths curriculum.

When discussing the maths curriculum with colleagues in your school, it would not be unusual to hear your fellow teachers discuss concrete, pictorial and abstract (CPA) when they are talking about curriculum delivery (see Figure 7.1). The maths curriculum can contain many abstract topics and when children are introduced to these first in a concrete and hands-on manner, this will lay the foundation of their understanding before moving on to pictorial representations and then abstract symbols/representations. The inspiration for this approach to teaching maths is that CPA is a key component of maths teaching in many high-achieving Asian countries (influenced by the research of Bruner). Sequencing the learning of more abstract elements of the curriculum to move from concrete to abstract will support the children we teach to establish a deeper understanding of maths.

You will be able to read more about CPA in the signposts to additional resources at the end of this chapter.

When you look at the primary maths curriculum, you will notice that each page has 'statutory requirements' and 'notes and guidance (non-statutory)'. Whilst the guidance and notes are not a legal requirement, it is advised to not ignore this aspect of the maths curriculum as it can be useful, particularly to the novice teacher, in helping understand how to teach some of the statutory materials. Many schools use a scheme of learning to support the teaching of maths, so ensure you familiarise yourself with the design of this scheme and how your school uses it.

Another important aspect of the maths curriculum is the progression of calculation within the curriculum. As teachers, we need to ensure we are teaching our children the most efficient and accurate methods for calculation as they progress through the curriculum. For example, by the end of Key Stage 1, children should be able to count up and down in 1s, 2s, 5s and 10s, and they build on this counting in Key Stage 2 where they learn to be able to count up and down in multiples of 3s, 4s, 6s, 7s, 8s, 9s, 11s, 12s, 25s, 50s, 100s and 1000s (this will include negative numbers). We would want children to be able to do this quickly, mentally and without relying on written methods. On the other hand, we would also expect our children to develop fluency in their written methods and by the time they leave KS2, they should be confident in efficiently using these methods

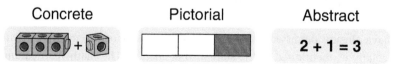

Figure 7.1 An illustration of the CPA approach

for addition, subtraction, multiplication and division. There is a useful appendix as part of the curriculum document which provides some examples of formal written methods which you can familiarise yourself with. Your school will also have a calculation policy which will help you understand what method you teach in each year group/phase.

How Do you Build Subject Knowledge?

For some of us, we will not have studied maths since our GCSEs and the subject knowledge may initially appear intimidating. It is, however, our job to ensure we have the specialised content knowledge as well as the pedagogical knowledge to teach maths effectively.

The starting point to developing your subject knowledge is identifying gaps in your own knowledge and planning steps to address these.

A good starting point is reading the national curriculum for maths. Start with the Year 6 content and explore the statutory requirements for number and place value; addition, subtraction, multiplication and division; fractions; ratio and proportion; algebra; measurement; geometry; and statistics. In which aspect is your subject knowledge strongest? Which area do you need to develop? Look at each bullet point in the curriculum to guide your thinking.

Children in Year 6 also sit statutory Key Stage 2 assessments (often referred to as SATs), and sitting and self-marking some of these papers will support you in developing your subject knowledge. These test papers can all be found for free online.

As well as ensuring your subject knowledge is secure, you will need strong pedagogical knowledge. We have referenced research at the start of this chapter which guides you towards some of the research-informed pedagogical choices you could make. There is much debate around the best pedagogical choices in maths, but here are some points for you to consider:

- What concrete, pictorial and abstract resources will I use? Am I using these because I think I must use them or are they supporting the learning in the classroom?
- What mathematical vocabulary am I teaching in this unit? Can I confidently explain what these words mean?
- Will all learners be able to access what I am teaching? What scaffolds will I provide for those learners who need them?
- What calculation method(s) will I be using? Ensure you can confidently use and explain your method(s) (it/they may be different from the method you learnt when you were in school!).
- Once I have identified what I want the children to learn in maths, how will I break it down into small, manageable steps?

- What resources will I use to support the children's learning? Ensure these resources are supporting the learning and not distracting from it.

Summary

We have discussed in this chapter:

- Maths is one of the few statutory subjects across all primary key stages, emphasising the importance of maths for young children.
- A high-quality maths curriculum must be well sequenced and start in the early years. The national curriculum for maths outlines, year by year, what children should learn across the primary phase. New learning builds on previous learning.
- It is essential that we have a secure subject knowledge to be able to teach the content of the curriculum, as well as knowledge of the best pedagogical choices for maths.

Signposts to Additional Resources

The first point to note about resources and maths is that your school will most likely be using a scheme or an approach to teaching maths, so you must familiarise yourself with this.

As we have previously mentioned, the use of concrete resources supports pupils' development and understanding of more abstract concepts. Speak with the maths leader and find out what concrete maths resources are available within your school – for example, Key Stage 1 and EYFS may use a resource called 'numicon' to provide concrete support for children.

There is a wealth of resources available online for supporting the teaching of primary maths, but to help you focus in on some high-quality ones we recommend the following:

- National Centre for Excellence in the Teaching of Mathematics – www.ncetm.org.uk
- A free booklet on the use of manipulates to support CPA teaching – https://thirdspacelearning.com/blog/concrete-pictorial-abstract-maths-cpa
- The EEF on supporting Key Stage 1 maths – https://educationendowment foundation.org.uk/education-evidence/guidance-reports/early-maths
- The EEF on supporting Key Stage 2 maths – https://educationendowment foundation.org.uk/education-evidence/guidance-reports/maths-ks-2-3
- A teaching maths in primary schools guidance document – www.gov.uk/government/publications/teaching-mathematics-in-primary-schools –

━━━━━ QUESTIONS TO ASK EXPERTS ━━━━━

The Initial Teaching Training Core Content Framework (DfE, 2019a) specifies that during your training year you need to have input from experts. Here are some maths curriculum questions you could ask when you get the opportunity to meet the maths leader in your school:

- Can you help me understand the thinking behind the maths curriculum for this school?
- What resources do we use in this school to support the teaching of maths?
- How is concrete, pictorial, abstract (CPA) used as part of the school's curriculum?
- I am working in Year X - how might I understand what the children have already been taught in maths?

Discussion Questions

1 In small groups, read the early learning goals for mathematics. Discuss what our youngest children learn about maths.
2 Look at appendix 1 of the maths curriculum (examples of formal writing methods for addition, subtraction, multiplication and division). How are these strategies different/ similar to the methods you were taught?
3 In small groups, read the three aims of the mathematics curriculum (on the first page). Do you feel these are reasonable expectations by the end of KS2?
4 Which area of maths do you want to learn more about to secure your subject knowledge? How will you do this?

8

SCIENCE

Why Teach Science to Primary Children?

The discipline of science helps young children to make sense of the world around them. Scientific understanding provides a foundation for children to observe, question, analyse, process and ultimately challenge. Knowing why things occur and how things work provides powerful knowledge with in which children can challenge, question and ultimately envisage a different future.

Science can empower children to think in different ways, analytically, critically and creatively. Science requires us to look closely, to consider what we see, to use our knowledge to make predictions, to reflect on different options, to test our assumptions, to look for evidence that support our theories, to communicate what we know, and so much more. Introducing children to primary science is essential for them to gain independence of thought.

The important work of laying foundations in science begins during a child's early years. Young children notice colours, patterns, and changes from watching their ice lolly melt on a hot day to finding an empty bird's egg. Interaction with the world around them and then the powerful questioning that follows on from observation are the beginning of scientific thinking. Within the early learning goals for the end of reception (DfE, 2022b), there are clear aims relating to science within 'Understanding the World', one of the seven areas of learning. The science curriculum itself may start in Key Stage 1, but it is essential that we know how children transition from the Early Years Foundation Stage, as they bring valuable knowledge and understanding with them as they move to Year 1.

For primary children, we can offer an insight into the world of science through subject content and also by introducing them to the work of scientists themselves. We truly are standing on the shoulders of giants, as the scientist Sir Isaac Newton famously wrote (Newton, 1675). We can teach primary children about the work of scientists so that they can understand the processes scientists go through, what questions they ask, what methods they employ. We do this so that pupils understand the discipline of science. So often, scientists are pictured in lab coats with crazy hair, blowing up a substance in a test tube. We do a disservice to the discipline if that is all children know of scientists and their work. In today's rapidly changing world, science can offer vital explanations of the issues we face, from climate change to food security to vaccines. Not only can it explain what is happening but it can suggest alternative futures. If we, as teachers, can foster an interest in science whilst developing a sound foundation of subject knowledge for our primary pupils, we can set them up with the freedom to pursue science through their secondary education and beyond. Ultimately, a love of science offers a deep understanding of the world we live in now and of what that world might become.

At primary level, there is no statutory assessment for science. Whilst English and maths are both assessed through Standard Aptitude Tests, known as SATs, towards the end of KS1 and KS2, science is assessed internally by teachers, using the school's own assessment systems. Many schools seek external validation of the quality of science in their institution through accreditation processes such as the Primary Science Quality Mark (www.psqm.org.uk), which includes professional development for teachers who lead science within their school. The government conducts a KS2 science test in a sample of schools bi-annually as a way of monitoring performance nationally. The outcomes from these sample tests, alongside reports from The Wellcome Trust (2017, 2020), paint a bleak picture of the quality of science in primary school. In 2019, the Standards and Testing Agency reported its findings from the tests taken by pupils in June 2018. The Agency found that 21.2% of children were working at the expected level in science. It also found that pupils who registered for free school meals and those who spoke English as an additional language, performed significantly worse than their peers (Standards and Testing Agency, 2019).

Primary science teaching needs a revolution and we can be a part of making that happen. We can secure our subject knowledge so that we can teach clearly and anticipate misconceptions. When we know science content well and fully understand it, we can be explicit with our teaching, equipping pupils with the vocabulary, knowledge and skills they need to be successful. We can ensure our science curriculum is sequenced effectively to provide a solid foundation for learning.

Key Elements of the Primary Science Curriculum

The primary science curriculum introduces children to foundational science knowledge and skills in biology, physics and chemistry. The curriculum should help children to understand and explain what they see in the world around them, encourage them to look closely and ask questions, and equip them with ways of finding answers. Within science, we have specified content in the curriculum alongside an additional important element, 'working scientifically'. This strand is woven through the science curriculum; it does not stand alone and must not be separated from the content within the curriculum.

An integral part of the discipline of science, 'working scientifically' encourages children to seek patterns, identify, classify, group, compare, test and research. It also introduces children to the idea that scientists work to answer questions through collecting, analysing and communicating data. Understanding the ways in which scientists work helps young children to see that scientific discoveries are not just suddenly made with a whizz and a bang, but are the result of a systematic approach involving knowledge and skills. Some science lessons may have a more hands-on, practical element; a demonstration or a test children are undertaking using specific equipment. In all science lessons, children are working scientifically as they look for patterns, identify and classify, compare, test, and so on. Research from the Ogden Trust by Bianchi et al. (2021) has shown that children take part in 'fun' science activities and enjoy them, but fail to recall the key learning points. Children learn and remember more when undertaking practical science tasks if they have a strong foundation of knowledge first. It is sometimes tempting to 'wow' young children with science demonstrations in an effort to make the subject appear enjoyable, without considering whether children have established the knowledge they need to understand what they are observing.

Primary science requires careful thought about the knowledge and skills pupils are developing and how working scientifically is embedded within the learning process. This understanding of the discipline of science and how knowledge is constructed within it helps children to make a connection to science. It is this connection that will support future engagement with science and ultimately impact upon future achievement.

Table 8.1 Examples of working scientifically

	Key Stage 1 Example	Key Stage 2 Example
Observing over time	Grow some seeds and watch their progress, note down how the seed changes over time	Observe mould growing on a piece of bread, note down how the bread changes over time
Pattern seeking	Look for patterns in the age and height of children in our class. Is the oldest child the tallest?	Cut open some fruit and locate the seeds, seek patterns in the way the seeds are dispersed, e.g. plants with berries often rely on animals to eat and disperse seeds
Identifying	Name and describe animals from a range of habitats	Identify the planets in the solar system
Classifying	Classify things according to the following: alive, dead, never been alive	Classify animals as vertebrates or invertebrates, and then further classify vertebrates into classes (mammals, amphibians, fish, birds, reptiles)
Grouping	Group plants based on their features, e.g. flowering and non-flowering plants	Group rocks based on their properties
Comparative and fair testing	Compare what happens to seeds in different conditions, e.g. with and without water, with and without light	Test which materials make the most effective parachute
Researching	Find out about scientists such as George Washington Carver who studied plants and suggested ways to improve soil quality to help farmers.	Find out how our understanding of astronomy has changed over time.

How to Sequence Subject Knowledge

As we have said in previous chapters, sequencing subject knowledge means thinking carefully about the order in which we teach things. We want science knowledge to build over time, for children to be learning and remembering more as they work through the curriculum. The schema children hold will become increasingly complex as they learn the content of the curriculum. In this way, the order in which we teach science content matters.

We must think about sequencing, because by doing so we are striving to make our curriculum content meaningful and also helping children to remember what they have learned.

Science is thought of as a hierarchical subject. This means that there are certain things that must be understood in science before more challenging content can be learned. For example, within the National Curriculum children learn about the human body in each year group. This is the sequence of the content:

> EYFS: Within Physical Development (one of the three prime areas of learning) children are learning to use their bodies both in the area of gross motor (large movements) and fine motor (smaller movements). They learn how to negotiate space and obstacles, develop strength, balance and coordination when playing, run, jump, hop, etc. These are gross motor skills. They also learn to hold a pencil, use scissors, paintbrushes and cutlery. These are fine motor skills. Whilst children are developing in these areas, they will be exploring and testing what their bodies can do, learning vocabulary to describe parts of their bodies and will show understanding of the human body through their play. (DfE, 2022b)

Table 8.2 Example of how knowledge of the human body is sequenced in KS1 and KS2

Year 1	Basic parts of the human body Senses
Year 2	Basic needs of humans for survival Exercise, diet and hygiene Offspring
Year 3	Nutrition Bones and muscles
Year 4	Digestive system Types of teeth and their functions
Year 5	Changes as humans develop to old age
Year 6	Circulatory system Diet, exercise, drugs and lifestyle Transportation of nutrients and water within the human body

Source: DfE (2015)

As you can see from this example, the sequence of the content is hierarchical. It wouldn't be sensible to teach the circulatory system first, before children have learned about the basic parts of the body. In Year 6, when children learn about exercise and diet, they are building on knowledge of parts of the body from Year 1, exercise and diet in Year 2, bones and muscles in Year 3, digestion in Year 4 and how humans grow and age in Year 5. All of this prior knowledge provides a foundation from which children can learn and remember more.

Here is a second example of how subject knowledge is sequenced in science, this time using plants:

> EYFS: Within understanding the world, one of the specific areas of learning in Early Years, there is an Early Learning Goal (to be achieved by the end of

Reception) focused on the natural world. Within this Early Learning Goal, children are expected to explore the natural world around them, making observations and drawing pictures of animals and plants. This gives children the opportunity to learn names of plants, notice shapes and patterns and begin to understand growth and change. They will also know some similarities and differences between the natural world around them and contrasting environments, and understand changes in the natural world including the seasons. (DfE, 2022b)

Table 8.3 How knowledge of plants is sequenced in the National Curriculum

Year 1	Common wild and garden plants, including deciduous and evergreen trees Structure of flowering plants including trees
Year 2	Seeds and bulbs Requirements for plant growth
Year 3	Functions of the parts of flowering plants Requirements of plants for life and growth Water transportation in plants Life cycles of plants; pollination, seed formation and seed dispersal
Year 4	Classification of living things, including plants Identifying and naming a variety of living things in the local and wider environment Environmental change
Year 5	Reproduction in plants
Year 6	Classification of plants Evolution and adaptation in plants

Source: DfE (2015)

Table 8.3 shows how knowledge of plants is sequenced through the National Curriculum over time. What we as teachers need to do is to add a lot more detail to this structure. The National Curriculum requires us to teach Year 1 children about common wild and garden plants and trees, but it is then our responsibility to choose which plants and trees. It would make sense for us to choose those that the children will encounter in the playground or the local area. Within a coherent, sequenced curriculum, those plants and trees will be returned to in Year 2 and beyond, and crucially added to, allowing children to build a bank of knowledge of plants over time.

Working scientifically is an area of the science curriculum that also needs careful sequencing. The National Curriculum helps us to do this by identifying the skills that must be developed in KS1, lower KS2 and upper KS2. When we are teaching science, we need to think not only about the skills we are helping children to develop, but also about those they have already mastered and those they will develop in the future.

Table 8.4 Working scientifically

Working Scientifically		
Key Stage 1: Years 1 and 2	Lower Key Stage 2: Years 3 and 4	Upper Key Stage 2: Years 5 and 6
• asking simple questions and recognising that they can be answered in different ways • observing closely, using simple equipment performing simple tests • identifying and classifying • using their observations and ideas to suggest answers to questions • gathering and recording data to help in answering questions	• asking relevant questions and using different types of scientific enquiries to answer them • setting up simple practical enquiries, comparative and fair tests • making systematic and careful observations and, where appropriate, taking accurate measurements using standard units, using a range of equipment, including thermometers and data loggers • gathering, recording, classifying and presenting data in a variety of ways to help in answering questions • recording findings using simple scientific language, drawings, labelled diagrams, keys, bar charts, and tables • reporting on findings from enquiries, including oral and written explanations, displays or presentations of results and conclusions • using results to draw simple conclusions, make predictions for new values, suggest improvements and raise further questions • identifying differences, similarities or changes related to simple scientific ideas and processes • using straightforward scientific evidence to answer questions or to support their findings.	• planning different types of scientific enquiries to answer questions, including recognising and controlling variables where necessary • taking measurements, using a range of scientific equipment, with increasing accuracy and precision, taking repeat readings when appropriate • recording data and results of increasing complexity using scientific diagrams and labels, classification keys, tables, scatter graphs, bar and line graphs • using test results to make predictions to set up further comparative and fair tests • reporting and presenting findings from enquiries, including conclusions, causal relationships and explanations of and a degree of trust in results, in oral and written forms such as displays and other presentations • identifying scientific evidence that has been used to support or refute ideas or arguments

Source: DfE (2015)

How Do You Build Subject Knowledge?

In primary school, as is the case with other subjects, science is often taught by a non-specialist. As teachers, it is our responsibility to ensure we equip ourselves with the necessary subject knowledge we need to teach the science curriculum. We may need to clarify our own understanding, identify any misconceptions we have, and check we are prepared to teach accurately. We must be careful not to assume that since it is primary science, it is simple.

The Core Content Framework (DfE, 2019a) emphasises that secure subject knowledge helps teachers to motivate pupils and teach effectively. As with other subjects, it is vitally important that we develop our science subject knowledge so that we know the content of the curriculum well and can confidently deliver high-quality science teaching. Our subject knowledge will continue to develop over time and will often need adapting as new discoveries, new understanding or achievements are realised within the field of science. During our training, we can take important steps to recognise our own knowledge gaps and then to read and research the subject knowledge we need to secure.

When considering science subject knowledge, we need to be aware of two main areas: content knowledge and pedagogical knowledge. Within content knowledge, we have the core subject knowledge, for example the three different types of rock: metamorphic, igneous and sedimentary. We also have another important element of content knowledge that the National Curriculum identifies as 'working scientifically'. This strand of content knowledge looks at scientific methods, processes and skills – for instance, asking questions, observing closely, performing simple tests, identifying and classifying, using observations to suggest answers to questions, gathering and recording data. Then, within subject knowledge, we must also consider pedagogical knowledge, the knowledge of how we teach primary science. At this stage in teacher training, we are just beginning to learn how we teach, we are watching, gathering information, reading and reflecting upon our practice. Importantly, we must look to research-informed practice to find the best ways to teach primary science, and we must be continually reflecting upon our practice with a focus on improvement at every stage.

When considering how to build your subject knowledge in science, a subject knowledge audit is a good place to start. Once you've established the areas of science subject knowledge that might need work, you can begin to inform yourself through reading, watching documentaries and talking to subject leaders and experts. The National Curriculum specifies the content knowledge children should learn – this will support your own subject knowledge but is not sufficient in itself; you will need to read around the subject content you need to teach.

Example: In Year 4, the National Curriculum requires children to learn about changing states of matter. It is important that we are clear on the content knowledge we need in order to break down this content into small, manageable chunks for children to understand. So we need to know the properties of solids, liquids and gases. We need to know that water freezes at 0° and boils at 100°. We need to know that when freezing, water turns from a liquid to a solid and when boiling, turns from a liquid to a gas. We need to know what the processes of evaporation and condensation are and what role they play in the water cycle. Once we are secure in our own subject knowledge, we need to think about how we teach this:

- *What can we assume children will already know about changing state and how can we check this?* For example, have they ever left a chocolate bar in their pocket and noticed that it became soft when it warmed up? Have they played in the playground on a frosty morning, noticing frozen puddles or ice crystals on the fences?
- *What vocabulary will children need in order to describe the properties of solids, liquids and gases?* Words such as pool, pile, hard, pour, hold, container, melt and freeze may need to be explicitly taught, with their use in a sentence modelled clearly. We need to have clear definitions of the words we want children to know and use so that we explain their meanings accurately.
- *What will I demonstrate?* You may decide to demonstrate heating water and will need to consider mitigating any risks involved in this to ensure your classroom is safe for the children. When demonstrating, your subject knowledge is very important and will help your explanations be as clear as possible.
- *What will children do to explore or apply their learning?* This is when you can consider how children will work scientifically. Children might group and classify different materials by their state. They might explore how temperature affects a substance such as water. They might set up a way to observe evaporation and record the rate of evaporation over time. When you think about how children will explore, apply or deepen their learning, it is important to consider what it is you want children to remember. Introducing chocolate to a science lesson might be an excellent way to demonstrate heating and melting, but you must ensure the learning is clear and that children don't get distracted by the excitement of using chocolate and forget what it is you wanted them to learn.

To develop your own subject knowledge, you may want to look at online resources such as STEM Learning, BBC Bitesize, or Royal Society of Chemistry Steps into Science. Conversations with colleagues can be very helpful – try running through the technical science knowledge of a topic with another adult before teaching the lesson. Drawing diagrams for yourself, writing out definitions in your own words and annotating images with key words could help you to secure knowledge. Find out what works well for you and always strive to learn more.

Building science subject knowledge will help you teach content confidently and will also help you to understand how to break down science content and concepts for young children so that they may grasp the fundamentals of this fascinating and important subject.

Summary

What we have discussed in this chapter:

- For primary children, developing a love of science offers a deep understanding of the world we live in now and of what that world might become.
- There is no statutory assessment for science; schools use their own internal assessment systems.
- Nationally, reports and sampling have shown that the standards of primary science have declined in recent years.
- The National Curriculum sequences content for science, giving us guidance for each year group.
- We must ensure our subject knowledge is secure in order to teach successful science lessons.

Signposts to Additional Resources

There is a wealth of resources available online for supporting the teaching of primary science. To help you focus in on some high-quality ones, we recommend the following:

- The Association for Science Education – www.ase.org.uk
- The British Science Association – www.britishscienceassociation.org
- The Primary Science Teaching Trust – https://pstt.org.uk
- The Royal Society – https://royalsociety.org
- The Royal Society of Chemistry – https://edu.rsc.org/primary-science
- STEM Learning – www.stem.org.uk

There are also many online journals, blogs, and science teachers on Twitter.

QUESTIONS TO ASK EXPERTS

The Initial Teacher Training Core Content Framework (DfE, 2019a) specifies that during your training you need to have input from experts. Here are some science curriculum questions you could ask:

- How is our science curriculum structured?
- How can I find out what my class learned last year in science?
- What materials are available to help me prepare my science lessons?
- How do we support reading and vocabulary development in science?
- What do we expect children in the year I am working in to be able to do in science?

Discussion Questions

1   In small groups, read the Early Learning Goals for Understanding the World. Discuss what our youngest children learn about the world through a scientific lens.
2   In small groups, read the National Curriculum for Science in KS1 and KS2. How does knowledge build over time?
3   Why is sequencing content important in science?
4   Which areas of science do you want to learn more about to secure your subject knowledge? How will you do this, and what resources will you use?

9

HISTORY

Why Teach History to Primary Children?

> 'History's purpose isn't to comfort us. History doesn't exist to make us feel good, special, exceptional or magical. History is just history. It is not there as a place of greater safety.' (David Olusoga, in The Guardian, 2016)

History is the story of the past; of times gone by, catastrophes, discoveries, revolutions, wars, societies. It is the story of people who once lived. When taught badly, primary history has the potential to create in our minds a feeling of superiority – how people did things in the past was 'behind' and we do a much better job now, in modern times. We'd like to offer a different lens through which to view primary history – one of explanation. History has the power to help our children to understand the world they live in. It explains why things are and what led to the position we find ourselves in today. It helps us to understand decision making, recognise legacies and interpret events. Importantly, history offers a connection with what came before us. It is our responsibility, as teachers, to help children to establish a connection to their past. In doing so, we not only support their understanding of the past, but also aid their understanding of the world they live in and how it might have changed.

As the British historian, David Olusoga said, 'History's purpose isn't to comfort us' (*The Guardian*, 2016). When we embark upon the teaching of history, we can and should be pushed out of our comfort zone. We must challenge our perceptions, be aware of our own prejudices and ensure we tell a story of the past that pursues truth.

From the early years to the end of Key Stage 2, we can take children on a journey through the past that leads them from prehistory, where archaeologists must search in the ground for clues about what life was like, through history, when people began writing aspects of life down in records that can be studied and with conclusions drawn. Children may encounter important events, such as the eruption of Mount Vesuvius and the destruction of Pompeii, dates etched in our memories such as 1066 and the Battle of Hastings, concepts such as empire, trade, democracy and war, as relevant today as they were in the past. They will encounter people – those who fought for their rights, those who wanted to increase their power, those who created war or peace. As they learn about history, children will be developing chronological awareness. As teachers, we will support them to construct a mental timeline; a coherent narrative of the past.

The teaching of history requires careful thought, content-based choices and a vision for the big picture of what children will learn. The National Curriculum offers us some guidance on curriculum content, but we need to do some further thinking. If a specific period of time is to be taught, for example 'The Stone Age to the Iron Age', we need to think about what we include. This period spans 10,000 years of prehistory; what can we teach in a six-week unit? What is the essential knowledge and understanding we want pupils to take away from this time period? We will explore this theme further in the following section.

In many schools, history is taught under the umbrella of 'topic'. This approach can have its advantages in terms of time saving and creating cross-curricular links. However, it is important to recognise the uniqueness of the discipline of history and we urge caution with the topic approach. When teaching primary children history as a subject, we help them to establish an understanding of the identity of the discipline. They understand that history is the study of the past; they know about the work historians do to gather information, to interpret, to explain. Children can understand, for example, how the work of a historian may differ from that of a geographer or scientist.

History encourages those who study it to consider the importance of perspective. This is critical conceptual understanding for young children to develop over time. If they can ask themselves, 'Who is telling this story and where are they telling it from?', they can begin to think critically about the content they are studying. They can also begin to develop an understanding of multiple perspectives; how accounts of a single event may differ depending on the perspective of the person giving the account. Children can also begin to understand how history is contested; how the uncovering of new knowledge can challenge and build upon our understanding of the past.

Teaching history in primary school offers an insight into this fascinating discipline and, over time, we strive for children to develop a love of history that they can carry with them into their secondary education, continuing to be curious, to question, to argue, to reason and ultimately to understand.

How Is History Subject Knowledge Sequenced?

Sequencing subject knowledge in history simply means considering the order in which we teach history content. In primary school, it is often the case that children jump from time period to time period in no coherent order. Children might study the Greeks one year, then the Victorians in another, then the Romans in another. The result of this is a very muddled mental timeline and no understanding of how particular historical events gave rise to others. Chronology (the arrangement of dates and events in the order they happened) is a golden thread that must run through our primary history curriculum. However, a purely chronological history curriculum would be problematic.

If we tried to map our curriculum completely chronologically, it may look like this:

Early Years: Prehistory (Stone Age, Bronze Age, Iron Age)
KS1: Ancient History (Egyptians, Greeks, Romans)
KS2: Modern History (Industrial Revolution, WW1 and WW2)

The problem with this is that young children need to develop a conceptual understanding of what the past is before they can engage with any historical content in a meaningful way. When young children learn about dinosaurs, a popular topic in the early years (but not a National Curriculum requirement), they begin to understand that these creatures lived a very long time ago in the past, and they don't live now, in the present.

Children may also explore their own timeline, such as changes from when they were born to the present, as they work, in nursery and reception, towards the Early Learning Goal: Past and Present. As a child's mental timeline begins to establish, they can add to it, developing chronological understanding. As teachers, we can support this sequencing of events in our pupils' minds by consistently referring to timelines, even timelines of the day or week. Over time, as children learn and

Dinosaurs (past) ←————————————————————→ Me (Present)

Figure 9.1 Simple chronological understanding

remember more, they will populate their timeline with dates, events, people and places, and conceptually an understanding of change over time will grow.

Children will populate their mental timeline as they work through the primary curriculum, adding to it and refining it as they learn and remember more.

It is helpful to consider two different types of historical knowledge when we think about sequencing in history. **Substantive knowledge** in history is knowledge that is understood to be fact: dates, places, people, events. Substantive knowledge is that which we know, to the best of our ability, to be true.

Disciplinary knowledge is how that knowledge was established. In history, disciplinary knowledge requires an understanding of what historians do. For primary children, this means understanding that historians are people who study the past using sources. Historians ask questions, research, analyse, draw conclusions, and communicate their findings in reports. Although children won't be using the terms substantive and disciplinary knowledge, as teachers we are developing understanding of both for our pupils. As children learn more over time, they will understand how historians work and how that differs from the work of a scientist or a geographer or an artist.

Let's explore how we would sequence a KS2 unit of work in history on the Stone Age to the Iron Age.

What Do I Want My Children to Know and Be Able to Do at the End of This Unit?

The National Curriculum requires that children learn: Changes in Britain from the Stone Age to the Iron Age (DfE, 2013c).

This period of history spans over 10,000 years and we probably have around half a term to teach this. So, we need to think carefully about what we want the children to know and be able to do. We need to consider the chronology in this time period;

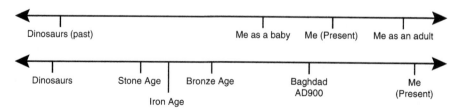

Figure 9.2 Chronological understanding developing over time

children need to be able to name and explain why the time periods are described as the Stone Age, Bronze Age and Iron Age. To grasp this fully, children need to know that our understanding of these times is based on the tools that people used, and therefore they also need to know what bronze and iron are. We might want to introduce some key vocabulary to describe times within this period, for example Neolithic, meaning new stone age (*neo* is the Greek word for new and lithic comes from *lithos*, meaning stone). In the Neolithic period, people began sharpening stones for tools, domesticating animals and settling in villages. Children need to know that this period is known as pre-history as there are no written records for this time; what we know comes from study of what was left behind by the people who lived then. We also need to focus on changes in Britain, so it would be useful to identify some key places associated with each age, such as Skara Brae in Scotland (a Stone Age settlement), and to think about how people lived in these places at the time we are studying.

Where Will I Start?

When we embark upon planning a sequenced unit of work in history, we need to reconnect children to their previous learning. For this unit, we want to ensure children have a developing understanding of chronology. You may want to ask yourself the following:

- What have children already studied in history in previous years? How can I connect this new learning to the previous learning?
- How can I check what children already understand about the past?
- What can I do to support those children in my class who have not yet secured an understanding of the past, present and future?

What Will My Sequence of Learning Look Like?

It makes sense for this unit to be taught in a sequence that reflects chronological order. It is, of course, not the only way to approach the teaching of this content, but here we shall unpick an example:

Step 1: An introduction to prehistoric Britain
Step 2: Life in the Stone Age (stone age tools, hunter-gatherers, and early farming)
Step 3: Skara Brae (a Stone Age settlement)
Step 4: Life in the Bronze Age (agriculture, carts with wheels, mining for metals, tools and weapons)

Step 5: Life in the Iron Age (settlements, hill forts, Celtic culture, weapons, jewellery)

Step 6: To complete this unit, children will write a historical report to answer the question: 'How did life in Britain change from the Stone Age to the Iron Age?'

*Steps may be one or more lessons depending on term length and timetabling.

What Does Progress Look Like Within This Unit?

Progress in primary history is not something we can just see and tick off. When looking for progress, we need to look for several elements under the umbrella of 'knowing more and being able to do more'. Within this unit that covers the Stone Age to the Iron Age, we are looking for the following:

- Are children using subject-specific *vocabulary*? As children progress through the lesson content, engaging with new concepts and ideas, they should be explicitly taught new vocabulary. We then need to build in frequent opportunities for them to use their newly acquired vocabulary within our lessons. As children become more experienced, they will use new words with more accuracy and confidence.
- Are children showing understanding of *chronology*? Can they use temporal connectives (words that join sentences or phrases together to indicate what time something is happening) when talking about the content of this unit? For example, '*After* the Stone Age, the *next* period of time is known as the Bronze Age'. Can children talk about changes over time in the period you are studying?
- Are children showing understanding of how knowledge of the past is established? As children progress through the history curriculum, they will build disciplinary knowledge. Within this unit, children will understand that during prehistoric times, events were not written down and recorded for us, but archaeologists can tell us about the past by studying things that were left behind. Children may be able to show their knowledge and understanding of the discipline of history as they talk about Skara Brae, what was found there and the conclusions that can be drawn from the artefacts. This will contribute to their developing understanding of how historians work and how knowledge within the subject of history is formed.

Early Years

In the early years, our youngest pupils will be introduced to history in a number of ways, for example through stories from the past, through pictures, through looking at maps from the past, and through talking to older people about the past. At the end of reception, children at the expected level of development will have achieved what is set out in the Early Learning Goal Understanding the World: Past and Present:

- Talk about the lives of the people around them and their roles in society
- Know some similarities and differences between things in the past and now, drawing on their experiences and what has been read in class
- Understand the past through settings, characters and events encountered in books read in class and storytelling. (DfE, 2022b)

It is vital that we recognise that children's historical understanding doesn't just begin in Year 1; children bring a range of experiences and knowledge with them from the early years and from home. Knowing the content of the early years curriculum is important for all teachers, even if they teach in KS1 or KS2, as it forms the foundation for future learning.

Elements of the History Curriculum

Within the history curriculum in primary school, children will learn the following elements of this discipline:

- a chronological history of Britain as a narrative (or story)
- history of the wider world (ancient civilisations and empires)
- understanding of abstract terms such as empire, civilisation, parliament
- historical concepts such as continuity and change, cause and consequence, significance
- historical enquiry (how historians use evidence (sources) to establish knowledge in history)
- historical perspective: understanding how local, regional, national and international history is connected.

When we approach a unit of work in history, we need to use these elements of history to form our plans. So we might be asking ourselves:

- What time period are we focusing upon? What do children already know that will help them to understand this? What happens within this time period?
- Where in the world is my unit focusing upon? Is this local, national, British or international history?
- Which historical terms do I need to teach explicitly and in context?
- Which historical concepts will my children grapple with?
- Which sources will my children encounter, and why and what will they understand?
- How can I link this learning to the rest of the curriculum to support children's historical perspective?

The National Curriculum requires children to 'think critically, weigh evidence, sift arguments and develop perspective and judgement' (DfE, 2013c). We need to be aware that these skills do not exist in a vacuum; they are the embodiment of a strong knowledge base. In simple terms, you can't think critically about something you know nothing about. Developing perspective is something a child can do if they have strong foundational knowledge. So, it is imperative that we are clear about what exactly we want children to know and remember, and therefore what we teach.

The National Curriculum divides history into Key Stage 1 (Years 1 and 2) and Key Stage 2 (Years 3–6). In Key Stage 1, children are introduced to historical content and time periods that will be studied in more detail in Key Stage 2. The National Curriculum is not purely chronological; it introduces history in Key Stage 1 in a more general way, with children expected to learn about changes within living memory, events from beyond living memory, significant individuals and significant historical events, people and places in their local area (DfE, 2013c). Then, moving into Key Stage 2, children explore periods of history, including:

- the Stone Age to the Iron Age in Britain
- the Roman Empire and its impact on Britain
- Britain's settlement by Anglo-Saxons and Scots
- the Viking and Anglo-Saxon struggle for England
- a local history study
- an aspect or a theme in British history that extends chronological knowledge beyond 1066
- ancient civilisations (schools can choose from Ancient Sumer, the Indus Valley, Ancient Egypt, the Shang Dynasty of Ancient China)
- Ancient Greece (Greek life, achievements and their influence on the western world)
- a non-European society that provides contrasts with British history (schools can choose from Islamic civilisation including Baghdad in AD900, Mayan civilisation in AD900, or Benin in AD900–1300). (DfE, 2013c)

Schools assign these periods of history to specific year groups within Key Stage 2 and decide how to allocate curriculum time to each area of study.

Sequencing within the history curriculum has two important aspects: the sequencing of the history curriculum overall and the sequencing of content within an individual unit. As a trainee or an early career teacher (ECT), you need to be most concerned with the sequencing within an individual unit and then have an awareness of where the unit you are teaching fits in with the rest of the curriculum. For example, if you are responsible for teaching 'Ancient Greece' and you know your class studied 'Ancient Egypt' the year before, you can familiarise yourself with what exactly they studied and check to see what has been remembered. Then you can make the connections to their previous learning about the Ancient Egyptians explicit when introducing the Ancient Greeks. Then, within your unit of study of Ancient Greece, you can think about the sequence of learning, what progress looks like and what children should know and be able to do by the end of the unit.

Sometimes teachers fall into the trap of 'doing' a history topic, so you might hear 'Oh, we've done the Romans' as if a six-week unit in Year 4 is everything children ever need to know about the Romans. Any subject matter, such as 'the Romans', could be studied by a 7-year-old or a 77-year-old, by a primary child or a PhD student. Avoid thinking about history content as being 'done' and ticked off, never to be revisited again. Rather, shift your thinking towards what children know and can do in history. Consider your activities carefully: What are children thinking about when they are completing an activity? Is this activity helping them to secure their understanding? Is it asking them to think in the way a historian would think? Always come back to what you want children to remember.

If you are on a placement or begin your career in a free school or an academy, the institution may have chosen to use its curriculum freedoms to create a history curriculum that does not follow the National Curriculum. In this case, you may want to look at the history curriculum you have and explore the following:

- How is history introduced in the early years and Key Stage 1?
- How does the curriculum approach chronology? (Which time periods do children learn about and in which order are they studied?)
- Which significant people do children learn about through the curriculum?
- Which areas of local, British and world history are studied?
- Which sources do pupils encounter and what do they learn about their significance?

How Do You Build Subject Knowledge?

As we have mentioned previously, we have a responsibility to teach a wide number of subjects with a wide knowledge base, and history is a good example of this. Historians tend to focus on specific periods of history and develop specific knowledge and expertise for these times. In each of the areas covered by the National Curriculum in History, we must have the specialised *content knowledge* required to teach the subject well, without necessarily being specialists ourselves. We also need *pedagogical knowledge* – knowledge of how we teach history and what research tells us about best practice.

It is our responsibility to recognise our own knowledge gaps and fill them by reading, researching and informing ourselves. If we are expected to teach children about the Ancient Greeks, we need to know what exactly we are teaching and read around the subject. The journey of our own learning will be ongoing throughout our teaching career, but at this early stage whilst training, it is important to identify areas that we need to focus on. Reading the National Curriculum is an essential way to familiarise yourself with subject content, but, as we have said before, it won't teach you what you need to know as a teacher.

Early Islamic civilisation, including Baghdad in AD900, is one of the options a school might choose to study for a non-European society that provides contrast with British history. If you have good subject knowledge in this area, you'll be able to identify some important people, such as Caliph Al-Mansur who founded the city of Baghdad, known as the 'city of peace' based on a circular shape, or Caliph Harun al-Rashid who founded the House of Wisdom, a centre of scholarship that, in AD900, housed the largest library in the world. But if you are not experienced in this area, you will need to do some research and find out how the story you will tell your children unfolds. You will need to identify which people, places, dates and events are key to understanding more about this period of time. Your school may have curriculum plans or schemes of work to help you, but improving your own subject knowledge is vital and something experienced teachers continue to do throughout their career. Seek advice from subject leaders, where possible, and make use of resources such as subject associations and museums to ensure you have accurate content. Our subject knowledge audit in the appendix of this book will help you to focus in on your own knowledge and to identify areas to work on. We need to read books and news articles, watch documentaries and inform ourselves, so that we can, to the best of our abilities, be the expert in the classroom. The internet is littered with errors and misinformation, so always ensure you are using reputable and trustworthy sources. Building our subject knowledge helps us to become the expert in the room and helps us to ignite children's interest and passion for history.

Whilst we are working on our subject knowledge, we must also consider pedagogical knowledge. This is concerned with the 'how' of teaching history. When we've secured what we want children to learn about, we need to think about *how* we will teach them. There are many different approaches to classroom pedagogy, and it is important we think deeply about what effective learning looks like in the different subjects we teach. As we have said, when you begin to look into this, you will find many debates and disagreements, and sometimes it is hard to separate opinion from fact. Often, pedagogical approaches are taken because they 'feel right', not necessarily because an evidence base has shown they are the best bet for making learning happen. Pedagogy is a huge area that cannot be covered in a meaningful way in this chapter, but here are some points to consider for history:

- How will I provide an opportunity to reconnect to prior learning? For example, show a timeline with sections blanked out, show a map with parts missing, display a source or artefact, ask children to match key vocabulary to definitions, discuss a misconception.

- How will I explicitly teach the key vocabulary? For example, oral rehearsal, discussing etymology, looking for other words that are linked to the key word, identifying roots of words, putting key words in a sentence.
- Once I have identified what I want the children to learn in history, how will I break it down into small, manageable chunks, ensuring children are not overloaded? What am I saying? What am I showing the children? Are they listening, watching, reading, and is that what I want them to do?
- What teaching resources will I use to support children's learning? For example, sources, texts, maps, images, photographs, diagrams, videos.

Summary

What we have discussed in this chapter:

- Primary history offers children the chance to understand the world they live in.
- A high-quality history curriculum is well sequenced and clearly identifies what the children will learn from EYFS to KS2. This clarity helps teachers to teach effective history lessons and helps children to learn and remember more.
- Our own knowledge of both the history subject content (what we teach) and the pedagogy (how we teach) is crucial and will develop throughout our teaching career.

Signposts to Additional Resources

There is a wealth of resources available online for supporting the teaching of primary history, but to help you focus in on some high-quality ones we recommend the following:

- BBC Bitesize – www.bbc.co.uk/bitesize
- The British Museum – www.britishmuseum.org
- The Historical Association – www.history.org.uk

═══════ QUESTIONS TO ASK EXPERTS ═══════

The Initial Teacher Training Core Content Framework (DfE, 2019a) specifies that during your training you need to have input from experts. Here are some history curriculum questions you could ask when you have the chance:

- Can you help me to understand the thinking behind the history curriculum?
- What materials are available to help me prepare my history lessons?
- Which periods of history will children learn about in the key stage I am working in?
- What do we expect children in the year I am working in to be able to do in history?

Discussion Questions

1 In small groups, read the Early Learning Goals for Understanding the World. Discuss what our youngest children learn about the past.
2 In small groups, read the National Curriculum for history in Key Stage 1 and Key Stage 2. How does knowledge build over time?
3 How can we develop chronological understanding for our pupils?
4 Which areas of history do you want to learn more about to secure your subject knowledge? How will you do this, and what will you use?

10

GEOGRAPHY

Why Teach Geography to Primary Children?

> 'The study of geography is about more than just memorising places on a map.
> It's about understanding the complexity of our world, appreciating the diversity
> of cultures that exists across continents. And in the end, it's about using all that
> knowledge to help bridge divides and bring people together.' (Barack Obama, 2012,
> National Geographic GeoBee) (www.politico.com/blogs/politico44/2012/05/
> obama-asks-geography-bee-question-124490)

Primary geography is a subject of huge significance in our changing world. You
only have to flick through the news headlines to see stories of war, economic
crash, famine, and environmental destruction. We live in a global world of many
divisions, unequal wealth and social challenges. The pupils we teach will be the
consumers, the innovators, the decision makers of tomorrow and they have a fundamental right to knowledge of the world around them. Geography looks closely

at how humans interact with the world, how landscapes shape our behaviour and how our actions change our environment. When we work within the discipline of geography, we ask and answer some of life's big questions: who are we, where are we going, where do we fit in? Geography can provide a space for our pupils to explore who they are, where they may go and who they may become.

Obama's quote above makes an important point that geography is more than memorising places on a map. We want children to appreciate the **diversity** of cultures that exist across continents. We want children to know about places and people so they can connect to them, understand them and bridge divides. However, fundamentally this appreciation of diversity cannot exist in a vacuum; you have to know lots in order to recognise and appreciate diversity. You have to have memorised many places on maps, or at least have secured knowledge of many places around the world if you are to appreciate diversity. The more we know, the more connections we can make between places, people and processes. So yes, geography is about more than memorising places, but those places must be memorised in the first place.

As trainee teachers, we must think carefully about how we provide a high-quality geography education that equips pupils with knowledge and understanding that foster curiosity about the world, creating a springboard for future learning. As pupils progress through their primary geography curriculum, they will be building knowledge, deepening understanding and developing geographical skills. Over time, pupils will not only know more, but they will be able to do more in geography. This might mean they can talk in more detail about more places, interpret different types of maps, and draw conclusions after looking at some geographical data. We teach geography so that pupils can better understand their local, national and international environments, and ultimately can participate in the change happening around them.

Ofsted published a research review focused on primary geography in 2021 (Ofsted, 2021b), which looks at the available research in geography education and identifies what a high-quality geography education looks like. Sadly, the research shows that geography is not being taught well at primary level; it suffers from low status and a decline in time allocated to it (Ofsted, 2021b). Keeping this in mind as we enter the profession is important, as we have the power to address this.

The Ofsted research review in geography found the following which are important for teaching students to consider (Ofsted, 2021b):

- High-quality geography is taught by teachers with good subject knowledge (we will look at this in more detail later in this chapter).
- A high-quality geography curriculum is sequenced well and clearly identifies what the children will learn; this helps children to learn and remember more.
- Locational and place knowledge is important and helps pupils to locate features, navigate successfully and make the link between a location and geographical processes.

- Using maps effectively enables children to present spatially organised data and to analyse it using their geographical knowledge. They need frequent opportunities to practise this, including in fieldwork.
- Teachers must use accurate assessment to ensure pupils have learned the content of the curriculum, and the outcomes of assessment should be used to adapt the curriculum where necessary.

To summarise, here is what the research review showed:

- Our own subject knowledge is very important.
- We need to identify and understand what we want the children to learn and in what order they should learn it.
- Children need to learn where places are and what happens in these places, using maps and fieldwork to support their learning.
- We must check that children are learning and remembering more over time.

How Is Geography Subject Knowledge Sequenced?

Sequencing subject knowledge in geography means thinking carefully about the order in which we teach things. Like we would do in mathematics, in geography we want knowledge to build over time. As pupils work through the sequenced curriculum, we want to see them asking and answering increasingly complex questions, building and using a wide geographic vocabulary. Over time, pupils will learn more and remember more in geography. We are building increasingly complex schema in pupils' minds, adding to their knowledge and deepening their understanding.

It is helpful to look at two forms of subject knowledge in geography: substantive and disciplinary knowledge. *Substantive* knowledge is the substance of geography, the content, the places, the features, the processes, it's the 'what' in 'what you have to learn'. Substantive geography knowledge is what we know about the world. *Disciplinary* knowledge is *how* the knowledge we have in geography has been constructed or revealed. This brings in an important element of understanding: how do geographers find out about the world? Understanding what geographers do, what fieldwork they may undertake, what questions they may ask about a place, all help children to develop disciplinary understanding in geography. Thinking about these two forms of knowledge and how they are woven through the curriculum, can help us to understand how children make progress in geography.

The order in which our curriculum content is taught matters. Although there may be no consensus, no perfect way in which to order the knowledge in the geography curriculum, thinking about sequencing helps us to break down what we want to teach into small, manageable chunks. It helps us to think about what children need to understand first – for example, an understanding of aerial perspective is useful for them to grasp what maps represent. So, if you are faced with the task of planning a unit of geography, these things will be useful to consider.

Let us now look at an example for a Key Stage 1 unit on the UK.

What Do I Want My Children to Know and Be Able to Do at the End of This Unit?

I want them to know and be able to locate the countries of the UK. I want them to be able to identify the UK on a map of the world. I want them to recognise the Union Jack. I want them to use geographical terminology to describe the UK, including words such as island, coast, mountain, compass directions. I'd also like them to know where we live in relation to the rest of the country.

Where Will I Start?

I will think about what they may already know about the UK and maps. I will find out what they have learned previously and I will ask them questions to help them remember what they learned before. I will think about those children who have had more experience with maps and who have good geographical understanding developing already, and those who may have had much less experience. I will think about what the children with less experience need to learn to close the knowledge gap.

What Will My Sequence of Learning Look Like?

I will break down the knowledge content so that I am introducing new knowledge in small, manageable chunks. My sequence of learning may look like this:

- Step 1: Reconnect to prior learning, and introduce countries of the UK and the Union Jack. Familiarise children with an atlas; locate a map of the UK and discuss the islands of the UK.
- Step 2: Focus on the physical geographical features of the UK using examples from different countries of the UK, e.g. Lochs and Munros in Scotland, Brecon Beacons in Wales, Peak District in England, The Giant's Causeway in Northern Ireland. Talk about how we know about these places, and what geographers can tell us about them.

- Step 3: Focus on coastlines, given the UK is made up of many islands, name the bodies of water that surround the UK, build vocabulary, e.g. cliff, beach, erosion, sand. Discuss what a geographer might say about coastlines.
- Step 4: Focus on the human geography of the UK: where do people live? Teach names of capital cities of the UK. Begin to develop an understanding that people live in places that suit their needs.
- Step 5: Focus on our local area, where it is located in the UK, and human and physical geographical features of the local area. Discuss how a geographer would describe our local area.
- Step 6: Using their knowledge, children will write a report about the UK. (I might use some of my English lesson time to teach children how to structure a report.)

*Each step may take up one lesson or more than one lesson.

What Does Progress Look Like Within This Unit?

When we look for progress, we look for a number of things under the umbrella of 'knowing more and being able to do more'. For the example given here, we are looking for children to do some of the following:

- be able to recognise a map of the UK and point out places they know and recognise
- be able to describe the landscape of the UK using some geographical vocabulary including compass directions
- be able to use an atlas, using the contents page and/or index, where necessary, to locate the map they need.

At the end of this unit, I want my children to be able to talk about the UK in much more detail than they could at the beginning. I want to see their interest growing and I want to see them making more connections. For instance, they might notice the Union Jack when watching a clip of the Olympics.

When sequencing our curriculum content, we think about what children have already learned, what we want them to learn and where they will take their learning next. It is helpful to familiarise yourself with expectations for the previous year and for the year following the one you are teaching in.

Let us look at an outline of how locational knowledge progresses through Key Stages 1 and 2.

Key Stage 1:

- Name and locate continents and oceans.
- Name, locate and identify the characteristics of the four countries and capital cities of the UK.

Key Stage 2:

- Countries of the world with a focus on Europe, North and South America, focus on environmental regions, key physical and human characteristics, countries and major cities
- Counties and cities of the UK, human and physical characteristics, key topographical features, land use patterns and how these have changed over time
- Latitude, longitude, Equator, Northern and Southern Hemisphere, Tropics of Cancer and Capricorn, Arctic and Antarctic Circle, Prime/Greenwich Meridian and time zones.

Early Years

In the early years, the youngest pupils in the schools we teach in will encounter geography in a number of ways, perhaps through stories about contrasting environments, through pictures, through simple maps, through walking around the school grounds and placing locations in their minds. At the end of reception, children at the expected level of development will have achieved what is set out in the Early Learning Goal, Understanding the World: People, Culture and Communities:

- Describe their immediate environment using knowledge from observation, discussion, stories, non-fiction texts and maps.
- Know some similarities and differences between different religious and cultural communities in this country, drawing on their experiences and what has been read in class.
- Explain some similarities and differences between life in this country and life in other countries, drawing on knowledge from stories, non-fiction texts and – when appropriate – maps. (DfE, 2021)

Key Elements of the Geography Curriculum

This important foundation of subject knowledge is the beginning of the geography education the pupils will receive in school. They will be beginning to think about diverse places, comparing them with their local area, noticing similarities and differences. They will be developing a sense of space and place through looking at aerial views and maps, conceptually beginning to understand that a map is a representation of an area of land or sea. They might be starting to realise the purpose of a map and how maps can be used to show routes in familiar areas or from storytelling. Importantly, they will have the opportunity within the early years to explore, to play and to learn new vocabulary, which will help them to identify, name and talk about places, people and environments.

As pupils progress over time through Key Stages 1 and 2, they will know more and remember more about their local area, the UK and the world. This could look like them recognising places on maps, asking questions about what it might be like to live in a place, telling you interesting things about different countries and making connections between features of their local area and other areas.

The National Curriculum structures the subject of geography into the following areas: locational knowledge, place knowledge, human and physical geography, and geographical skills and fieldwork. Locational knowledge is about naming, locating and identifying the characteristics of continents, oceans and countries. Over time, pupils will be able to identify and describe more places around the world as their knowledge builds. In Key Stage 1, they locate the seven continents and five oceans and also study the UK and its surrounding seas. In Key Stage 2, pupils build on this knowledge, studying Europe, North and South America, and the UK in more detail. Children also become familiar with geographical terms such as latitude, longitude, the Tropics of Cancer and Capricorn, The Prime/Greenwich Meridian and time zones. This knowledge helps children to understand what information a globe holds and how a geographer would use their knowledge of the world, and it helps them to make connections – for example, if a child understands the curve of the earth, the equator, the tropics and the North and South Pole, they will be able to connect the location of a country with the climate they'd expect it to have.

Place knowledge in the National Curriculum requires pupils to understand similarities and differences in the world through studying specific areas. In Key Stage 1, pupils study a small area of the UK and a small area of a contrasting non-European country. In Key Stage 2, they extend their knowledge of the diversity of earth through studying a region of the UK, a region in a European country and a region within North or South America.

In both Key Stage 1 and Key Stage 2, pupils are developing their knowledge and understanding of physical and human geography. Physical geography looks at the surface of the earth and its features. Human geography looks at people and how they interact with the earth. Both branches of geography deal with the important concept of interconnection: how natural and human phenomena are related, and how one impacts the other.

Within the National Curriculum, pupils study seasons, weather and the location of hot and cold areas of the world. Pupils will become familiar with geographical vocabulary that identifies and describes human and physical features of the world, for example beach, river, soil, city, farm, port. As pupils progress through Key Stage 2, their understanding of human and physical geography will grow, building on their prior knowledge from Key Stage 1. They will study key aspects of physical and human geography, including climate zones, biomes, rivers, the water cycle, settlements, trade and the distribution of natural resources.

Geographical skills and fieldwork feature in both Key Stages 1 and 2 in the National Curriculum. Pupils must be using maps, atlases and globes throughout their primary geography education. When pupils use an atlas frequently, they become familiar with it, know how to use it and become 'atlas literate'. This means that when they are searching for information in an atlas, they know where to look. They can interpret and understand the information maps hold, and use them to find out more about places. They can rise to challenges such as: 'East Anglia is flat. Prove it.' This will show how they can use their knowledge of the atlas to find a relief map of the East of England.

Fieldwork is a vital part of a geography curriculum in primary school. With the logistics of taking children off-site, sometimes the key purpose of the fieldwork can get lost amongst risk assessments, packed lunchboxes and transportation. It is important to be clear on the geographical skills and understanding the field-work will provide. This simple framework is useful when considering the purpose of fieldwork:

- Collect: What are we trying to find out? What sort of data would help us to find answers? How will we collect that data?
- Represent: Once we've collected data, what can we do with it? Do we need to organise it in a way that helps it to be easily understood? Do we need to represent data in graphs?
- Interpret: What does our data show us? Did we answer the question we set out to? How do we need to communicate our findings? What next steps will we take as a result of our findings?

As they work through the curriculum, pupils will be taught and will apply geography skills such as using compass directions, using locational and directional language, map drawing and interpreting symbols from a key. These skills are developed in Key Stage 2 when pupils use digital mapping, grid references and ordnance survey maps.

If you are on a placement or begin your career in a free school or an academy, the institution may have chosen to use its curriculum freedoms to create a geography curriculum that does not follow the National Curriculum. In this case, you may want to look at the geography curriculum you have and explore the following:

- How does locational knowledge build through the curriculum?
- How is my geography curriculum sequenced so that children learn more and remember more over time?
- How do geography skills such as map reading develop over time?
- What place knowledge will my pupils already have? What place knowledge do I need to teach? What place knowledge will they learn about in the forthcoming years?
- What geographic fieldwork will my pupils need to engage with and how can I facilitate this?

How Do You Build Subject Knowledge?

As primary teachers, it is our responsibility to teach a wide number of subjects with a wide knowledge base. We jump from teaching children to read and write in the morning, to teaching them how to throw and catch a ball in the afternoon. In each of the subject areas we teach, we must have the specialised *content knowledge* required to teach the subject well, but without necessarily being specialists ourselves. We also need *pedagogical knowledge* – the knowledge of how we teach geography and what research tells us about best practice.

Although we may be teaching subjects we haven't studied since our own secondary education, we must ensure we know the content of the curriculum well. It is our responsibility to recognise our own knowledge gaps and fill them by reading, researching and informing ourselves. The journey of our own learning will be ongoing throughout our teaching career, but at this early stage whilst training, it is important to identify areas that we need to focus on. So, if you haven't studied geography since early on in secondary school, that might be a good place to start. Reading the National Curriculum is an essential way to familiarise yourself with subject content, but it won't teach you what you need to know as a teacher. It specifies that children must know the seven continents and five oceans in Key Stage 1, but we must check first that we know what they are.

The subject knowledge audit in the appendix of this book will help you to focus in on your own knowledge and to identify areas to work on. In simple terms, we need to find out what we need to know (using the National Curriculum as a guide), identify what we don't know and then learn about it. We need to read books and news articles, watch documentaries and inform ourselves, so that we can, to the best of our ability, be the expert in the classroom. This helps our own confidence, but also helps us to ignite children's interest in and passion for geography.

Let us look at an example: If you've not heard the words 'topographical features' before or are unsure what they mean, find out. Etymology (the study of word origins) helps us to understand the meaning of the word 'topography' – it comes from the Greek *topographia*, from *topos*, meaning place and *graphia*, meaning writing. Topography refers to the arrangement of physical features of an area. Topography describes an area or place, including both human and physical features. A topographical feature might be a hill, mountain, valley, cliff, bridge or road. Someone describing the topography of a place might also mention its elevation – how high the land is from sea level. Topography is important because it tells us about a place and we might use that information to make decisions about a place – for instance, is this place suitable for farming? Can new homes be built in this place? Is this place likely to flood? What environmental issues might this place face?

As students and then as qualified teachers, we must keep working on our subject knowledge. Like the children we teach, we can add to our schema, deepening our understanding over time. Building subject knowledge will help us teach content confidently and will also help us to understand how to break down the content and concepts to help young children understand.

Whilst we are working on our subject knowledge, we must also consider pedagogical knowledge. This is concerned with the 'how' of teaching – if we've secured what we want children to learn about, we need to think about how we will teach them. There are many different approaches to pedagogy and it is important that we think deeply about what effective learning looks like. When you begin to look into this, you will find many debates and disagreements; sometimes it is hard to separate opinion from fact. Often, pedagogical approaches are taken because they 'feel right', not necessarily because an evidence base has shown they are the best bet for making learning happen. Pedagogy is a huge area that cannot be covered in a meaningful way in this chapter, but here are some points to consider:

- How will I give an opportunity to reconnect to prior learning? For example, show a blank map, show a map with parts missing, show a graph, show a diagram, ask children to match key vocabulary to definitions, discuss a misconception.
- How will I explicitly teach the key vocabulary? For example, oral rehearsal, discussing etymology, looking for other words that are linked to the key word, identifying roots of words, putting key words in a sentence.
- Once I have identified what I want the children to learn in geography, how will I break it down into small, manageable chunks, ensuring children are not overloaded? What am I saying? What am I showing the children? Are they listening, watching, reading, and is that what I want them to do?
- What teaching resources will I use to support children's learning? For example, atlases, maps, globes, a compass, aerial views, photographs, diagrams, graphs, videos.

Summary

What we have discussed in this chapter:

- Primary geography offers a chance for our children to learn about the world, who they are and how the world around them is changing.
- A high-quality geography curriculum is well sequenced and clearly identifies what the children will learn from EYFS to KS2. This clarity helps teachers to teach effective geography lessons and helps children to learn and remember more.
- Our own knowledge of both geography subject content (what we teach) and pedagogy (how we teach) is crucial and will develop throughout our teaching career.

Signposts to Additional Resources

If we had to choose one resource you will need to teach primary geography, it would be an atlas. Some schools are well resourced in this area, whilst others are not. So, when you are on your teaching practice or in a classroom of your own, find out what atlas provision the school has. Ideally, you will have a class set of atlases for children to use regularly, but if the atlases are shared between classes, make sure you know where they are and think about when you will need them. The more frequently children use an atlas, the more easily they will navigate around it and the more confident they will become at locating the information they need. Check how old the atlases you have are, and if they are old, watch out for changes to country names and borders. There are atlases more suitable for Key Stage 1, slightly smaller, larger print and easier to navigate. If you have the opportunity to use these in Key Stage 1 and a 'junior' atlas in Key Stage 2, that would be ideal. However, any atlas is fascinating for children and a vital tool for supporting teaching and learning.

There is a wealth of resources available online for supporting the teaching of primary geography, but to help you focus in on some high-quality ones we recommend the following:

- Digimap (a really useful online mapping tool) – https://digimapforschools. edina.ac.uk
- The Geography Association – www.geography.org.uk
- Ordnance Survey (the UK's national mapping agency) –www.ordnancesurvey. co.uk/education
- The Royal Geographical Society – www.rgs.org/schools/teaching-resources/ developing-primary-geography

━━━━━ QUESTIONS TO ASK EXPERTS ━━━━━

The Initial Teacher Training Core Content Framework (DfE, 2019a) specifies that during your training you need to have input from experts. Here are some geography curriculum questions you could ask when you have the chance:

- Can you help me to understand the thinking behind the geography curriculum?
- What materials are available to help me prepare my geography lessons?
- Which places will children learn about in the key stage I am working in?
- What do we expect children in the year I am working in to be able to do in geography?

Discussion Questions

1 In small groups, read the Early Learning Goals for Understanding the World. Discuss what our youngest children learn about the world.
2 In small groups, read the National Curriculum for geography in Key Stage 1 and Key Stage 2. How does knowledge build over time?
3 Why is sequencing content important in geography?
4 Which areas of geography do you want to learn more about to secure your subject knowledge? How will you do this, and what will you use?

11

ART

Why Teach Art to Primary Children?

Art in its many forms has been created by humans for many thousands of years. Archaeologists have found drawings of pigs on cave walls on the Indonesian island of Sulawesi that they believe to be over 45,000 years old. What these prehistoric people were intending, we cannot know, but they made marks on the walls of the caves to represent something that they had a mental picture of, something from the world around them. They communicated, expressed, left a lasting message, and thousands of years later we can take meaning from this.

Defining art is not a simple task – it is not the study of a particular aspect of the world, it is not a subject with clear boundaries, but it is an innately human activity. Art has been created by people for many different reasons: to express emotion, for its beauty, to represent, to show religious devotion, to tell stories. Artists may create for themselves, as a form of self-expression, to bring their thoughts into the world, or they may create for other people, to communicate meaning in a way that words cannot. Though we may struggle with a clear definition, we can say that art involves creating, expressing and communicating.

For us as teachers, we must consider what the journey through the art curriculum will look like for our children. How do we best introduce our children to the wonders of art as a subject? Within primary school, art has two main areas to focus upon: the understanding of art and artists, and children's own ability to create art. It is important we help children to understand that artists rarely create masterpieces in one sitting. An artist would practise and refine their skills over time. So, a child working through the art curriculum should have frequent opportunities to build their knowledge and skills, returning to previously learned skills to practise and master them. Within the art curriculum, we want children to encounter artists and to look closely at the work they produce. So, we must make choices about which artists we will include in the curriculum and what children will learn from them.

In school, children can sometimes think of art as something you are 'good at' or not. Children, particularly older children, are often reluctant to make marks on their paper for fear of 'getting it wrong'. They may be disappointed with their efforts if their artwork doesn't look how they imagined it would. Therefore, we must, as primary teachers, do two important things: explicitly teach the skills required to draw, paint and sculpt, whilst also giving children space to develop those skills in an environment that supports practice and individual growth. As non-specialists, we may have our own concerns about our artistic skills, but it is important that we show a positive attitude towards art and be willing to explore, experiment and grow, just as an artist would.

Throughout the primary art curriculum, children will encounter a range of artists, including painters and sculptors from different times, countries and contexts. The selecting of the artists in our curriculum requires careful consideration. We must look beyond the obvious to include a diverse range of artists who show that art is created worldwide by many different people. As we have mentioned in previous chapters, we want our children to see themselves reflected in the curriculum we teach, so teachers must be encouraged to make thoughtful choices about the artists our children learn about.

The teaching of art requires careful thought, content-based choices and a vision for the big picture of what children will learn. The National Curriculum offers us some guidance on curriculum content, but it is not as detailed as other subjects such as science. As teachers, we need to do some further thinking to create a meaningful art curriculum that helps children develop their own skills of expression and different forms of art, whilst learning from the great artists of our time.

In many schools, art is taught under the umbrella of 'a topic'. Art is often added to a topic because a certain artist has produced art that links to it, for example studying Van Gogh's *Sunflowers* when the class topic is 'plants'. The problem with adding art to topics, although it may add a creative dimension that children will enjoy, is that the sequencing of art content is often neglected. Within art and design, children need to develop their artistic skills over time, for example using a pencil to create the effect of texture in a drawing, or using colour to create the effect of light. As we have discussed in the other subject areas, in art and design children need to know more and remember more over time. If they know how to create texture in a drawing using a pencil, they can improve on this skill over time as they practise it in different contexts. If they do this once and never return to it, it is much harder to improve. When teaching primary children art as a subject, with sequenced curriculum content that builds and gets more challenging over time, we can support our pupils to become better artists, better designers, better creators.

Art encourages those who study it to consider the importance of perspective. What was happening when this piece of art was created? What was the artist experiencing at this time? If children can ask themselves, 'Who is telling this story and where are they telling it from?', they can begin to think critically about the artistic content they are studying. With design, children can think about the influences a designer has reflected in their work, looking beyond what they see in front of them, to think about style.

Teaching art in primary school offers an insight into this fascinating discipline and, over time, we strive for children to develop a love of art that they can carry with them into their secondary education, continuing to be curious, to question, to argue, to reason and ultimately to understand.

How Is Art Subject Knowledge Sequenced?

Sequencing subject knowledge in art simply means considering the order in which we teach art content. The National Curriculum does not prescribe a sequence of learning for art and design, but it outlines areas to cover including drawing, painting and sculpture. It mentions 'other art and design techniques' which could include, for example, photography, textiles, printmaking or film. The National Curriculum goes on to specify that children must learn about the work of a range of artists, craft makers and designers but does not specify which, or what about them must be learned. Often, primary schools will follow an art scheme of work they have purchased, or one they have developed themselves. It is important to make sure that the content of the art curriculum we work with has sequenced content, so that children are taught how to be skilled at drawing, painting, sculpting or whichever artistic technique they are learning. This approach helps children to develop an appreciation of both art and design techniques and the work of artists. Sequencing this content helps us to make sure that children learn and can do more as they work through the art and design curriculum.

Within an art curriculum, there should be a core of substantive knowledge. This means understanding the main elements of art: line, colour, shape, form, tone, space and texture. When we put these elements together, they form the design of a work of art. Understanding these elements helps children to look closely at artwork and consider how an artist has used the elements of art in their work. Substantive knowledge in art also includes key artists and pieces of artwork that children can recognise and discuss. Within art, disciplinary knowledge is the knowledge of how artists work, how art is created, and how art can be appreciated, studied and critiqued. Disciplinary knowledge in art is important for children to understand the many ways that art features in the world, the many ways artists work and the different purposes of art. It also helps children to engage with the processes of creating art: using the imagination; analysis, investigation and exploration; design and planning; and evaluation. These are integral ways in which artists work.

Creating a connection to artists helps children to see themselves in the roles that artists may hold and to develop ambition and aspiration to work in the field of art. In simple terms, if a child knows how an artist works, they might believe they could one day do the same.

Let's explore how we would sequence a Key Stage 1 unit of work in art on line.

What Do I Want My Children to Know and Be Able to Do at the End of This Unit?

In KS1, the National Curriculum requires that children learn:

- to use a range of materials creatively to design and make products
- to use *drawing*, painting and sculpture to develop and share their ideas, experiences and imagination
- to develop a wide range of art and design techniques in using colour, pattern, texture, *line*, shape, form and space
- about the work of a range of artists, craft makers and designers, describing the differences and similarities between different practices and disciplines, and making links to their own work. (DfE, 2013a)

Where Will I Start?

When we embark upon planning a sequenced unit of work in art, we need to reconnect children to their previous learning.

You may want to ask yourself the following:

- What have children already studied in art in previous years? How can I connect this new learning to the previous learning?

- How can I check what children can already do and what they understand about how artists work?
- What can I do to support children in my class who need more fine motor support to enable them to become skilled with drawing lines?

We then need to consider our sequence of learning: what art skill will be explicitly taught, what practice will look like and which artists or works of art pupils will look closely at.

What Will My Sequence of Learning Look Like?

It makes sense for this unit on 'line' to develop sequentially, supporting children to learn and remember more. It is, of course, not the only way to approach the teaching of this content, but here we shall unpick an example:

Step 1: Prior learning; a task to find out what children can do

Step 2: Looking at how Miro uses line in his art

Step 3: Model drawing different types of line

Step 4: Practice: line drawings of shapes, regular and irregular

Step 5: Creating a Miro-inspired piece of art (an expression of the child's own understanding)

Step 6: Assessment task

*Steps may be one or more lessons, depending on term length and timetabling.

What Does Progress Look Like Within This Unit?

Progress in primary art is not something that is easy to measure with a simple test. When looking for progress, we need to seek out several elements under the umbrella of 'knowing more and being able to do more.' Within this unit that covers line, we are looking for the following:

- Are children using subject-specific vocabulary? As children progress through the lesson content, engaging with new artistic techniques and ideas, they should be explicitly taught new vocabulary. They can then use this new vocabulary in discussions about the work of artists or their own developing art. As children become more experienced, they will use new words with more accuracy and confidence.
- Are children able to look closely at a piece of art and think about how the artist has used lines?

- Are children showing an understanding of how to create different lines? They may have drawn different lines in their sketchbook, practising lines such as straight, curved, zigzag, looped, etc.
- Are children able to use their knowledge and skills to create their own art?

Using sketchbooks is a good way to observe progress over time as children develop the skills they need in art. Working in a sketchbook helps children to see all of the component parts that come together in their artwork.

Early Years

In the early years, our youngest pupils will be introduced to art in a number of ways, for example through painting, colour mixing, drawing, hand painting, finger painting, printing, and so on. At the end of reception, children at the expected level of development will have achieved what is set out in the Early Learning Goal, Expressive Arts and Design: Creating with Materials.

Children at the expected level of development will:

- safely use and explore a variety of materials, tools and techniques, experimenting with colour, design, texture, form and function
- share their creations, explaining the process they have used
- make use of props and materials when role-playing characters in narratives and stories. (DfE, 2022b)

It is vital we recognise that children's understanding of art doesn't just begin in Year 1; children bring a range of experiences and knowledge with them from early years and from home. Knowing the content of the early years curriculum is important for all teachers, even if they teach in Key Stage 1 or 2, as we must know what our children are expected to have mastered in early years. If staff in early years have taught children some basic colour mixing skills, these can be used in Year 1 and learning can be taken on to the next stage, rather than the Year 1 teacher needing to start from scratch. Early years is the *foundation* stage and a house built up on firm foundations will stand strong.

Key Elements of the Art Curriculum

Within the art curriculum in primary school, children will learn the following elements of this discipline: drawing, painting and sculpture.

When we approach our art curriculum, we need to use these elements of art to form our plans. So we might be asking ourselves:

- What are the steps a child needs to take to get better at drawing?
- What do I need to model to support children's understanding of painting techniques?
- How do sculptors plan and create their work and how can our children follow this method to create their own sculpture?

The National Curriculum divides art into Key Stage 1 (Years 1 and 2) and Key Stage 2 (Years 3–6).

In Key Stage 1, children should be taught:

- to use a range of materials creatively to design and make products
- to use *drawing*, painting and sculpture to develop and share their ideas, experiences and imagination
- to develop a wide range of art and design techniques in using colour, pattern, texture, *line*, shape, form and space
- about the work of a range of artists, craft makers and designers, describing the differences and similarities between different practices and disciplines, and making links to their own work.

In Key Stage 2, children should be taught:

- to create sketchbooks to record their observations and use them to review and revisit ideas
- to improve their mastery of art and design techniques, including drawing, painting and sculpture with a range of materials (e.g. pencil, charcoal, paint, clay)
- about great artists, architects and designers in history. (DfE, 2013a)

Schools assign these elements of art to specific year groups within Key Stage 2 and decide how to allocate curriculum time to each area of study.

Sequencing within the art curriculum has two important aspects: the sequencing of the art curriculum overall and the sequencing of content within an individual unit. As a trainee or as an ECT, you need to be most concerned with the sequencing within an individual unit and then have awareness of where the unit you are teaching fits in with the rest of the curriculum.

Sometimes teachers fall into the trap of 'doing' an art topic, so you might hear 'Oh, we've done Van Gogh so don't do him again' as if Van Gogh need only be studied the once. Any art subject matter, such as a particular artist, technique or movement could be studied at any age and any level of expertise. Avoid thinking about art content as being 'done' and ticked off, never to be revisited again. Rather, shift your thinking towards what children know and can do in art. Think about time given for children to develop their knowledge, understanding and skills. Always come back to what you want children to remember and be able to do to feel successful in art.

If you are on a placement or begin your career in a free school or an academy, the institution may have chosen to use its curriculum freedoms to create an art curriculum that does not follow the National Curriculum. In this case, you may want to look at the art curriculum you have and explore the following:

- How is art introduced in the early years and Key Stage 1?
- How does the curriculum develop skills over time? For example, line – when do children focus on their line drawings and how do they improve their skills over time?
- Which significant artists do children learn about through the curriculum?
- What different styles of art are studied and when?

How Do You Build Subject Knowledge?

As we have mentioned previously, we have a responsibility to teach a wide number of subjects with a wide knowledge base, and art is a good example of this. Artists tend to focus on specific styles or areas of art and develop specific knowledge and expertise. In each of the areas covered by the National Curriculum in Art, we must have the specialised *content knowledge* required to teach the subject well, without necessarily being specialists ourselves. We also need *pedagogical knowledge* – knowledge of how to teach art and what research tells us about best practice.

It is our responsibility to recognise our own knowledge gaps and fill them by reading, researching and practising our own skills. The journey of our own learning will be ongoing throughout our teaching career, but at this early stage whilst training, it is important to identify areas that we need to focus on. Take time to read the National Curriculum but, as we have said before, it won't teach you what you need to know as a teacher. Seek advice from subject leaders where possible, if you can, arrange to watch them teach art and make use of resources such as subject associations and galleries which often have an education arm to support teachers. The subject knowledge audit in the appendix of this book will help you to focus in on your own knowledge and to identify areas to work on. As with other subjects in primary school, building your subject knowledge helps you to become the expert in the room and helps you to equip our children with the skills they need to engage with and enjoy art.

As we have previously mentioned, alongside the development of our own subject knowledge, we must also consider pedagogical knowledge. This is concerned with the 'how' of teaching art. When we've secured what we want children to learn about, we need to think about *how* we will teach them. There are many different approaches to classroom pedagogy, and it is important that we think deeply about what effective learning looks like in the different subjects we teach. Pedagogy is a huge area that cannot be covered in a meaningful way in this chapter, but here are some points to consider for art:

- How will I give an opportunity to reconnect to prior learning? For example, what art skills have children been taught before? Which artists do they recognise?
- How will I explicitly teach the key vocabulary? For example, oral rehearsal, discussing etymology, looking for other words that are linked to the key word, identifying roots of words, putting key words in a sentence.
- Once I have identified what I want the children to learn in art, how will I break it down into small, manageable chunks, ensuring children are not overloaded? What am I saying? What am I modelling for the children? Are they listening, copying, exploring, expressing, working independently, and is that what I want them to do?
- Which art materials will I use to support children's learning? For example, paint, chalk, pastel, clay, ink, pencil.

Summary

What we have discussed in this chapter:

- Primary art offers children the chance to develop skills of expression.
- A high-quality art curriculum is well sequenced and clearly identifies what the children will learn from EYFS to Key Stage 2. This clarity helps teachers to teach effective art lessons and helps children to learn, remember and be able to do more.
- Our own knowledge of both art subject content (what we teach) and pedagogy (how we teach) is crucial and will develop throughout our teaching career.

Signposts to Additional Resources

There is a wealth of resources available online for supporting the teaching of primary art, but to help you focus in on some high-quality ones, we recommend the following:

- Access Art – www.accessart.org.uk/art-in-primary-schools
- The National Gallery – www.nationalgallery.org.uk/learning
- The National Society for Education in Art and Design – www.nsead.org
- The Metropolitan Museum of Art – www.metmuseum.org
- The Tate Gallery – www.tate.org.uk

━━━━━━ QUESTIONS TO ASK EXPERTS ━━━━━━

The Initial Teacher Training Core Content Framework (DfE, 2019a) specifies that during your training you need to have input from experts. Here are some art curriculum questions you could ask when you have the chance:

- Can you help me to understand the thinking behind the art curriculum?
- What materials are available to help me prepare my art lessons?
- Which artists will children learn about in the key stage I am working in?
- What do we expect children in the year I am working in to be able to do in art?

Discussion Questions

1   In small groups, read the Early Learning Goals for Expressive Arts and Design. Discuss what our youngest children learn and do in art.
2   In small groups, read the National Curriculum for art in Key Stage 1 and Key Stage 2. How do knowledge and skills in art build over time?
3   How can we help our pupils develop confidence in art?
4   Which areas of art do you want to learn more about to secure your subject knowledge? How will you do this, and what resources will you use?

12

MUSIC

Why Teach Music to Primary Children?

'The language of music is common to all generations and nations; it is understood by everybody, since it is understood with the heart.' (Gioacchino Rossini in Zanolini, Biografia di Gioacchino Rossini, 1875, as cited in Crofton and Fraser, 1985)

As primary teachers, and possibly non-specialists, we must consider what the journey through the music curriculum will look like for our children. Will it be a series of disconnected experiences or a meaningfully sequenced introduction to the world of music? Within primary school, music has two main areas to focus upon: understanding of the technical aspects of music, and children's own ability to translate their ideas and feelings into musical sounds.

As was the case with art, in music it is important we help children to understand that composers rarely create musical masterpieces in one sitting; there is a process to follow. A composer or musician would practise and refine their skills over time. So, a child working through the music curriculum should have frequent opportunities to build their knowledge and skills. They should have many opportunities to return to previously learned skills to practise and master them. Within the music curriculum, we want children to encounter different pieces of music, different composers and musicians, and to listen closely to the music they produce. We must make important decisions about which types of music children will be taught, and which composers and musicians they will learn about. As we mentioned in the chapter on diversity and inclusion, it is important for children to see themselves in the curriculum. There is explicit reference in the music curriculum for children to learn music from a range of musicians and various traditions. We don't want to leave these decisions to chance.

Developing a music curriculum requires careful thought, content-based choices and a vision for the big picture of what children will learn and be able to do. The National Curriculum for Music offers us some guidance on curriculum content, and the Department for Education published the 'Model Music Curriculum' for KS1, KS2 and KS3 in 2021 (DfE, 2021b). Many schools will have a music scheme of work designed specifically for non-specialists to teach. Some schools make a choice to deliver music during teachers' planning and preparation time, using the services of a specialist. However, music goes beyond a single lesson per week in the primary classroom, and as teachers we must ensure we have good subject knowledge, even if music is not our specialism.

The primary music curriculum offers quite broad guidance for teachers – for example, in KS1 children should be taught to 'play tuned instruments musically' and it is up to schools to decide what the content of this might look like – What instruments will we teach? What context will we use to teach this? How will this be sequenced logically so that children achieve this by the end of KS1? This openness means that each school will have a different approach to developing musical knowledge in their curriculum, and as teachers we need to ensure that we teach a meaningful curriculum and do not leave it to chance that children will develop their musical knowledge.

How Is Music Subject Knowledge Sequenced?

The music curriculum for KS1 and KS2 is only two pages in length – you can see the content of this in the curriculum part of this chapter, but it is useful to note that the broadness of the curriculum statements mean that it is up to schools to decide how they will sequence this in small steps. Let's explore how we would sequence a KS1 unit of work in music.

What Do I Want My Children to Know and Be Able to Do at the End of This Unit?

In KS1, the National Curriculum requires that children learn to:

- use their voices expressively and creatively by singing songs and speaking chants and rhymes
- play tuned and untuned instruments musically
- listen with concentration and understanding to a range of high-quality live and recorded music
- experiment with, create, select and combine sounds using the interrelated dimensions of music. (DfE, 2013a)

Where Will I Start?

Let's look at the following end of KS1 statement: *use their voices expressively and creatively by singing songs and speaking chants and rhymes*, and think what this might look like sequenced across KS1.

When we embark upon planning a sequenced unit of work in music, we need to reconnect children to their previous learning.

You may want to ask yourself the following:

- What have children already studied in music in previous years? How can I connect this new learning to the previous learning? What songs did children learn in EYFS?
- What can I do to support children in my class who need more experience playing tuned and untuned instruments?

We then need to consider our sequence of learning:

- What songs will children know by the end of KS1?
- When will I introduce these songs and how do these build upon each other?
- How will I teach children to use their voices expressively and creatively? What will this look like and how will I support children to be able to achieve this?

What Will My Sequence of Learning Look Like?

It makes sense for this unit on singing to develop sequentially, supporting children to learn and remember more. It is, of course, not the only way to approach the teaching of this content, but here we shall unpick an example (this is across all of KS1):

Step 1: Children would be in Year 1 and we would reconnect with their existing singing experiences. I would reconnect with songs they know from
when they were in reception and introduce them to new songs and chants
which they would be able to remember. I would also teach the children
about good singing posture and model this for the children as well as providing feedback on their posture.

Step 2: Once children have learnt some new songs and have understood posture, I would now sing and ask the children to sing back to me – I would
sing both high and low. I would also teach the children to sing in unison
and ensure there is an agreed understanding of what this should sound
like. Lots of practice opportunities would be provided and I would find the
opportunity for children to perform this to an audience.

Step 3: As children progress through KS1, I would teach them more songs and
begin to support children to understand how the lyrics in songs can carry
meaning. I would continue to revisit what good posture looks like. I would
build on singing in unison and provide opportunities to develop singing in
parts.

Step 4: Children would develop their musical vocabulary in relation to singing.
For example, I would introduce the word *tempo* and expect children to use
the word when talking about how fast or slow a song is.

Step 5: Opportunities to perform and sing for an audience would be introduced
regularly and children would end KS1 with a concert, applying all the singing knowledge they have developed.

*The above are set out in steps across KS1 and would be broken down into
smaller steps over a number of lessons.

What Does Progress Look Like Within This Unit?

Progress in primary music is not something that is easy to measure with a simple
test. When looking for progress, we need to look for several elements under the
umbrella of 'knowing more and being able to do more'. Within this unit that covers
line, we are looking for the following:

- Are children using subject-specific vocabulary? As children progress through
the lesson content, engaging with new musical content and techniques,
they should be explicitly taught new vocabulary. They can then use this
new vocabulary in discussions about the work of musicians or their own
developing musicality. As children become more experienced, they will use
new words with more accuracy and confidence.

- Are children remembering the different songs they have been taught? Are children growing in their sophistication in their ability to discuss the meanings of some of these songs?
- Are children showing growing confidence in performance skills? When an opportunity to perform is provided, how is performing in Year 2 building upon Year 1?
- When you observe children singing, what progress can you see? Is their posture improved and fluent by the end of KS1? Are they singing in unison and rounds?

Early Years

In the early years, our youngest pupils will be introduced to music in a number of ways – for example, through singing, chanting, playing with instruments or other things that make sound, such as dry rice in a bottle, and moving to music. At the end of reception, children at the expected level of development will have achieved what is set out in the Early Learning Goal, Expressive Arts and Design: Being Imaginative and Expressive:

- Invent, adapt and recount narratives and stories with peers and their teacher
- Sing a range of well-known nursery rhymes and songs
- Perform songs, rhymes, poems and stories with others, and – when appropriate – try to move in time with music. (DfE, 2022b)

Children bring a range of musical experiences and knowledge with them from the early years and from home. Research shows that babies in the womb can hear sounds and can respond to their mother's voice, so musicality may even begin developing before a child is born (Vogelsang et al., 2022). The foundation stage can provide rich musical experiences for children that support their musicality and confidence, and that also help to develop self-regulation.

It is important for all teachers to understand the early years curriculum, even if they teach in Key Stage 1 or 2, as we must know what our children are expected to have mastered in early years. If staff in early years have taught children songs, rhymes and rhythms, these can be used in Year 1 and learning can be taken on to the next stage, rather than the Year 1 teacher assuming they are starting from scratch. As we have mentioned before, and it is certainly true for music, early years is the *foundation* stage and from a strong foundation, children will flourish. In the resources section at the end of this chapter, there is reference to a document which has been created specifically to support the development of music in EYFS; we recommend you read this if you wish to develop your knowledge of music within this phase.

Key Elements of the Music Curriculum

Within the music curriculum in primary school, children will learn the following elements of this discipline: singing, listening, composing and performing.

When we approach our music curriculum, we need to use these elements of music to form our plans. So we might be asking ourselves:

- What are the steps a child needs to take to make progress in singing?
- What do I need to model to support children's understanding of active listening?
- How do musicians create musical pieces and how can we follow that process?

The National Curriculum outlines the following:

In Key Stage 1, pupils should be taught to:

- use their voices expressively and creatively by singing songs and speaking chants and rhymes
- play tuned and untuned instruments musically
- listen with concentration and understanding to a range of high-quality live and recorded music
- experiment with, create, select and combine sounds using the interrelated dimensions of music.

In Key Stage 2, pupils should be taught to:

- play and perform in solo and ensemble contexts, using their voices and playing musical instruments with increasing accuracy, fluency, control and expression
- improvise and compose music for a range of purposes using the interrelated dimensions of music
- listen with attention to detail and recall sounds with increasing aural memory
- use and understand staff and other musical notations
- appreciate and understand a wide range of high-quality live and recorded music drawn from different traditions and from great composers and musicians
- develop an understanding of the history of music. (DfE, 2013a)

Schools assign these elements of music across KS1 and KS2 and decide how to allocate curriculum time to each area of study.

Sequencing within the music curriculum has two important aspects: the sequencing of the music curriculum overall and the sequencing of content within an individual unit. As a trainee or as an early career teacher (ECT), you need to be most concerned with the sequencing within an individual unit and then have an awareness of where the unit of music you are teaching fits in with the rest of the curriculum.

If you are on a placement or begin your career in a free school or an academy, the institution may have chosen to use its curriculum freedoms to create a music curriculum that does not follow the National Curriculum. In this case, you may want to look at the music curriculum you have and explore the following:

- How is music introduced in early years and Key Stage 1?
- How does the curriculum develop skills over time? For example, what songs should children in Key Stage 2 be able to sing and how is that different from Key Stage 1?
- Which significant composers and musicians do children learn about through the curriculum?
- What different genres of music are studied and when?

How Do You Build Subject Knowledge?

As we have mentioned previously, as primary teachers we have the responsibility to teach a wide number of subjects with a wide knowledge base. Many of us may not be music specialists, and yet we must equip ourselves with the knowledge and understanding needed to teach the foundations of a music curriculum. We must learn the specialised *content knowledge* required to teach music well and we also need *pedagogical knowledge* – knowledge of how we teach music and what research tells us about best practice. We must recognise our own knowledge gaps and fill them by reading, listening, researching and practising our own musical skills.

Take time to read the National Curriculum but, as we have said before, it won't teach you how to deliver quality music lessons. Seek advice from subject leaders or specialists where possible, and if you can, arrange to watch them teach music. The subject knowledge audit in the appendix of this book will help you to focus on your own knowledge and identify areas to work on. Many schools will follow a music scheme of work, so familiarise yourself with the contents of this explore any professional development opportunities that may be offered. As an early career teacher, some specific advice we would offer for you to learn about music includes the following:

- Music is language-rich – there is much music-specific language we need to know and understand in order to teach music to our classes. The model music curriculum includes a glossary for KS1 and KS2 – this provides clear definitions for the vocabulary we teach as part of the curriculum and is a good place to build your subject knowledge.
- The model music curriculum also provides a useful chronology of music over time; this will support you in building your knowledge of music from different periods.

- We need to be able to teach children how to play musical instruments, and the curriculum we teach will support us in understanding how we might teach this. However, there are many great resources available which can support you to start learning how to play an instrument (e.g. YouTube videos) and one we recommend to support you to learn the ukulele can be found here: https://coustii.com/ukulele-chords-beginners.
- Singing is at the heart of the curriculum, particularly in KS1, so we need to have knowledge of a range of different songs we can teach children. Sing Up offers a range of songs and free resources on its website, with the organisation offering a free trial to access some other resources (www.singup.org/free-resources).

Over time, we will develop pedagogical knowledge for the teaching of music in primary school. When we've secured what we want children to learn about in music, from singing to playing instruments, we need to think about *how* we will teach them. There are many different approaches to classroom pedagogy, and it is important we think deeply about what effective learning looks like in the different subjects we teach. For music, we will need to consider how we use our time carefully and realistically in order to allow children to experience music and to learn and develop their own musical skills. Here are some points to consider for music:

- How will I give an opportunity to reconnect to prior learning? For example, what music skills have children been taught before? Which pieces of music or styles do they recognise?
- How will I explicitly teach the key vocabulary? For example, oral rehearsal, discussing etymology, looking for other words that are linked to the key word, identifying roots of words, putting key words in a sentence.
- Once I have identified what I want the children to learn in music, how will I break it down into small, manageable chunks, ensuring children are not overloaded? What am I saying? What am I modelling for the children? Are they listening, copying, exploring, expressing, working independently, and is that what I want them to do?
- Teaching music requires careful consideration of how behaviour will be managed. Children will naturally be excited when they get to use resources in their lessons and we want them to keep this enthusiasm for music, but we also need to ensure their excitement does not become a barrier for teaching. Therefore, you might consider putting the resources out before the lesson but having them just out of research, for example you may sit them under the chair or at the end of each row – this means children can't play with them as you model and teach, but when it is time for them to use the resources they can access them quickly. Establishing routines for music lessons will be essential and you can use song to support this.

- Depending on what you are teaching in music, you will need to consider how you wish to lay out the classroom. For example, if the lesson being taught requires children to be holding instruments, is it best to sit them in a way which supports them to hold and rest their instrument when needed? Or, if they are singing, are they best sitting in a circle with no tables so they can stand when needed and you can see them all?
- Which musical resources will I use to support children's learning? For example, instruments, pieces of music, opportunities to perform, and so on. When you join your new school, it is worth spending some time exploring the resources available to support the teaching of music.

Summary

What we have discussed in this chapter:

- Primary music.
- That a high-quality music curriculum is well sequenced and clearly identifies what the children will learn from EYFS to Key Stage 2. This clarity helps teachers to teach effective music lessons and helps children to learn, remember and be able to do more.
- That our own knowledge of both music subject content (what we teach) and pedagogy (how we teach) is crucial and will develop throughout our teaching career.

Signposts to Additional Resources

There is a wealth of resources available online for supporting the teaching of primary music, but to help you focus in on some high-quality ones we recommend the following:

- Arts Council hubs: each school will have a music hub they can work with to support the teaching of music, and you can find your local music hub here – www.artscouncil.org.uk/developing-creativity-and-culture/children-and-young-people/music-education-hubs
- The BBC's Bring the Noise is a range of free resources to support the teaching of music – www.bbc.co.uk/teach/bring-the-noise
- The BBC Ten Piece introduces KS2 children to ten pieces of classical music, and provides the resources to teach them – www.bbc.co.uk/teach/ten-pieces
- The ISM trust has created a primary music toolkit to support the teaching of primary music – www.ismtrust.org/resources/primary-toolkit

- The Model Music Curriculum is a framework created by the Department for Education which outlines a framework for teaching music in KS1 and KS2 – https://assets.publishing.service.gov.uk/government/uploads/system/uploads/attachment_data/file/974366/Model_Music_Curriculum_Full.pdf
- Music Development Matters offers guidance for those teaching music in EYFS – https://network.youthmusic.org.uk/musical-development-matters

QUESTIONS TO ASK EXPERTS

The Initial Teacher Training Core Content Framework (DfE, 2019a) specifies that during your training you need to have input from experts. Here are some art curriculum questions you could ask when you have the chance:

- How is music taught at our school? Do we use a scheme of work?
- How does our curriculum for music include a diverse range of musicians and music?
- What do we expect children in the year I am working in to be able to do in music?
- What materials are available to help me prepare my music lessons?
- Which composers will children learn about in the Key Stage I am working in?
- How can I learn more about how to improve my teaching of music?
- What instrument do we teach all children?

Discussion Questions

1 In small groups, read the Early Learning Goals for Expressive Arts and Design. Discuss how our youngest children might experience music.
2 In small groups, read the National Curriculum for music in Key Stage 1 and Key Stage 2. How do knowledge and skills in music build over time?
3 How can we help our pupils grow in confidence when performing?
4 Which areas of music do you want to learn more about to secure your subject knowledge? How will you do this, and what resources will you use?

13

DESIGN TECHNOLOGY

This chapter will outline

- Why we teach design technology to primary children
- How to sequence design technology subject knowledge
- How to develop skills over time
- Key elements of the design technology curriculum
- How to build your own subject knowledge
- Signposts to additional resources

Why Teach Design Technology to Primary Children?

> 'The essence of design lies in the process of discovering a problem shared by many people and trying to solve it.' (Kenya Hara, Japanese graphic designer, curator and writer, creative director at Muji) (www.designersreviewofbooks.com/2009/03/designing-design/)

At the heart of design technology (DT) is a process of designing a solution to a problem. Design technology has important creative elements, but it is also technical; there are processes, mechanics and scientific understanding that feed into the subject. Importantly, when working within design technology, children are applying their knowledge and understanding to a problem to solve it in an effective way. They must think logically, creatively, imaginatively and practically.

Design technology plays an important role in industry. New and emerging technologies are changing the way we manufacture things through processes becoming automated with the assistance of robotics. It also plays an important role in sustainability and the effort to reduce our carbon footprint through designing and making recycled or reusable materials. Design technology has huge reach over many areas of our lives, from the way we communicate, through how we travel, what we wear, what we eat, to the impact we have on our planet.

It is important that primary school children are introduced to foundational knowledge, concepts and skills that form the subject of DT. Children might be making moving vehicles, designing and choosing materials to create a waterproof coat for a toy, designing and sewing a hand puppet to tell a story, or creating a healthy meal. DT is more than just making models; it is teaching children to follow a process that identifies a problem, then designs and makes a solution that can be assessed for its effectiveness and success.

As teachers, we must consider what the journey through the DT curriculum will look like for our children. How do we best introduce our children to design technology and how do we develop their knowledge and skills in this area? Within primary school, design technology focuses on supporting children to:

- develop the creative, technical and practical expertise needed to perform everyday tasks confidently and to participate successfully in an increasingly technological world
- build and apply a repertoire of knowledge, understanding and skills in order to design and make high-quality prototypes and products for a wide range of users
- critique, evaluate and test their ideas and products and the work of others
- understand and apply the principles of nutrition and learn how to cook. (DfE, 2013a)

So, as teachers, we need to ask ourselves what we are supporting children to do, make, evaluate and cook within DT. As they journey through the design technology curriculum, children will learn about the process of design: discover, define, develop and deliver (M. Hunter, The Design Council, 2015).

It is important we help children to understand that designers, like artists, don't create a finished product in one sitting. Designers follow a process where they research a problem or a need, define what that problem or need is, develop a solution and then deliver or create that solution.

Like artists, designers practise and refine their skills over time. So, a child working through the design technology curriculum should have frequent opportunities to build their knowledge and skills, returning to previously learned skills to practise and master them. Within the design technology curriculum, we want children to encounter designers and to look closely at the work they produce. So, we must make choices about which designers we will include in the curriculum and what children will learn from them.

Designers you might want to consider including in your curriculum include:

- Elsie Owusu, an architect whose work includes the refurbishment of the Supreme Court of the UK and Green Park Tube Station in London. She is the founding member of the Society of Black Architects.
- Dame Zaha Mohammad Hadid, an architect, artist and designer whose work includes the London Aquatics Centre (built for the 2012 Olympics) and the Guanzaou Opera House in China.
- Karim Rashid, a designer whose work includes furniture, lighting, packaging and many luxury goods. He is known for only wearing pink or white clothing.
- Sir James Dyson, an inventor and industrial designer who is best known for inventing the bagless vacuum cleaner.
- Zephyr Wright, a civil rights activist and chef who became the official White House Chef in 1963. Wright is thought to have inspired President Lyndon B. Johnson to sign the Civil Rights Act through her communication of her experiences of racism under the Jim Crow laws in the USA.
- Althea McNish, an artist and textile designer who designed fabrics for Liberty, Dior and Queen Elizabeth II.

The teaching of design technology at primary level requires decision making by teachers focused upon what children will design, what materials they will use and which skills they will develop. The National Curriculum offers us some guidance on curriculum content, but, like art, it is not very prescriptive. For example, in Key Stage 1 children are required to use their knowledge of healthy diets to prepare dishes. As teachers, we decide which dishes to prepare, which ingredients to use, and which cooking skills we will teach.

In many schools, DT will be an area of the curriculum that is taught in a block – for example, a few times a year spending each afternoon for a week on DT, rather than a lesson a week over a half term, each term. On a practical level, blocking DT allows pupils to focus on their design process fully, during a concentrated period. However, once the DT block has been completed, children may not do any specific DT for a significant portion of their year. As teachers, we can consider how we use and apply the knowledge and skills taught in DT across the curriculum to offer children frequent opportunities to revisit them.

As with other practical areas of the primary curriculum, it is important that we consider how we keep our pupils safe during design technology lessons. Your school will have a health and safety policy, but, as a teacher new to a school or to the profession, it is sensible to seek advice from a mentor or senior leader before teaching the practical elements of DT.

When teaching DT, we might be asking children to use food, electricity, mechanisms, things that are hot, or tools that might be sharp or pointed, therefore we must consider mitigating for any risks that might occur in our classrooms, from allergic reactions to cuts, burns or other injuries. A risk assessment is a document that identifies potential risks, for example the risk of a child burning themselves whilst using an oven, and highlights the steps taken to avoid them occurring. Do seek out any existing risk assessments within your school and identify whether you need to create a specific one for your task. It may seem like extra paperwork but keeping children safe is a priority. It is our responsibility as class teachers to ensure the classroom is calm and well organised, that children have a clear understanding of the rules and that steps have been taken to minimise risks during practical work in DT.

How Is Design Technology Subject Knowledge Sequenced?

Sequencing subject knowledge in design technology simply means considering the order in which we teach content. The National Curriculum does not prescribe a precise sequence of learning for design technology, but it does outline areas to cover in Key Stages 1 and 2 when designing and making, under the umbrella terms: design, make, evaluate, technical knowledge. The second element of this subject is cooking and nutrition.

Some primary schools will follow a design technology scheme of work they have purchased, whilst others will have one they developed themselves. It is important to make sure that the content of the design technology curriculum we work with has sequenced content, so that knowledge and skills build over time, fuelling creativity and developing a love of design and cooking. Sequencing curriculum content helps us to make sure children learn and can do more as they work through the design technology curriculum. For example, cooking in KS1 may need to focus on teaching culinary skills such as chopping, mixing and kneading. Some children will have had experience of this outside of school, perhaps at home, whilst others will have not. In upper KS2, children may not need so much focused teaching of these skills but may be able to apply them in a range of contexts to prepare and cook a dish they have designed.

Within the design technology curriculum, you will find both substantive knowledge – specific content knowledge such as tools used for cutting, mechanisms such as levers and wheels; and disciplinary knowledge – how a designer works, their thought processes, how they develop a product from the research phase to delivery. In some parts of DT lessons, you will be teaching substantive knowledge content; for example, how an axle is essential within a mechanism with a turning wheel, or how to draw a cross-sectional diagram. In other parts of DT lessons, you will be guiding children to follow a design process, to think like a designer, to ask questions as a designer would. This disciplinary thinking helps children to see that what they are learning in school is mirrored in the wider world. We can help children connect to the world of design, to see themselves in design-based roles that they may aspire to be in one day.

Let's explore how we would sequence a Key Stage 1 unit of work in DT on moving vehicles.

What Do I Want My Children to Know and Be Able to Do at the End of This Unit?

In KS1, the National Curriculum for DT stipulates the following for pupils:
   Design

- design purposeful, functional, appealing products for themselves and other users based on design criteria
- generate, develop, model and communicate their ideas through talking, drawing, templates, mock-ups and, where appropriate, information and communication technology.

   Make

- select from and use a range of tools and equipment to perform practical tasks (for example, cutting, shaping, joining and finishing)
- select from and use a wide range of materials and components, including construction materials, textiles and ingredients, according to their characteristics.

   Evaluate

- explore and evaluate a range of existing products
- evaluate their ideas and products against design criteria.

   Technical knowledge

- build structures, exploring how they can be made stronger, stiffer and more stable
- explore and use mechanisms (for example, levers, sliders, wheels and axles) in their products. (DfE, 2013a)

From this, we can see that a good DT curriculum would include opportunities for construction, for using textiles (including sewing) and for cooking. There is a separate section within the DT curriculum for cooking and nutrition. Focusing for this example on construction, we would want children to have the following opportunities:

- designing a product (a moving toy) based on design criteria
- generating and developing their ideas through talking, drawing templates and mock-ups
- making the product using a range of tools, equipment and materials (in this example, a wheel and axle mechanism)
- evaluating their product: did it meet the design criteria?

At the end of this unit, children will have the substantive knowledge of how to make a moving toy and they will have followed the process of designing and making, supporting their disciplinary understanding of how designers work.

Where Will I Start?

When we embark upon planning a sequenced unit of work in design technology, we need to reconnect children to their previous learning.

You may want to ask yourself the following:

- What have children already studied in previous years? How can I connect this new learning to the previous learning? What have they made before? What materials have they used before?
- How can I check what children can already do and what they understand about how designers work?
- What can I do to support children in my class who need more fine motor support to enable them to become skilled with cutting and fixing? (In other contexts, skills such as chopping, mixing and kneading might be relevant.)

We then need to consider our sequence of learning: what knowledge and skills require explicit teaching, what will practice look like and which designers will pupils encounter?

What Will My Sequence of Learning Look Like?

A sequence of learning in DT will not always look exactly the same but it could follow this structure:

Step 1: Prior learning – a task to find out what children know and can do.
   You might want to check on children's cutting skills or their knowledge of wheeled vehicles. This step may also include some research looking at existing moving toy vehicles.

Step 2: Design – children will ask, what problem are we trying to solve?
   They will think about the needs of the user of their product (it could be

themselves or other users). They will develop their own ideas through talking, drawing and writing. They may use IT to support their design.

Step 3: Make – teachers will model certain aspects of making the moving vehicle, e.g. fitting the axle and wheels. Teachers may also want to model safe use of equipment such as scissors, glue guns and saws. Children will select useful tools and equipment when making their moving vehicles. This step may require more than one 'lesson' and children may benefit from a block of time to complete the step.

Step 4: Evaluate – this step is a chance for children to reflect on their design process and their product, and to evaluate it against their design criteria.

Step 5: Assessment task.

*Steps may be one or more lessons depending on term length and timetabling.

What Does Progress Look Like Within This Unit?

Progress in primary design technology is not something that is easy to measure with a simple test. We can check on some of the substantive knowledge children are developing, for example we could ask children to draw and label a wheel and axle mechanism. We could explore their disciplinary understanding by asking children to explain why the design process is important, or what designers think about when they are designing a product. This would help us to see what children know and remember at the end of this unit. Within the unit, we might notice that children become more confident using tools, such as scissors, rulers and glue guns. They might have used a saw for the first time to cut their doweling rod to size for the axle, so we might have noticed their measuring and cutting skills developing.

As with other subjects, when looking for progress we need to look for several elements under the umbrella of 'knowing more and being able to do more' in design, making, evaluating and in children's developing technical knowledge. Within this unit that covers moving vehicles, we are looking for the following:

- Are children using subject-specific vocabulary? As children progress through the lesson content, engaging with new design techniques and with the mechanisms within their vehicles, they should be explicitly taught new vocabulary. They can then use this new vocabulary in discussions about the work of designers or their own design work.
- Are children able to study a moving toy vehicle and discuss how it has been designed?
- Are children able to generate and develop their own ideas, revising their ideas based on research?

- Are children able to make their design, using a range of materials?
- Can children talk about the strengths and challenges of their design?

Using workbooks or project books is a useful way of recording in design technology, using photographs alongside children's sketches, diagrams, plans and written articulation of the design process.

Early Years

In the early years, our youngest pupils will be introduced to elements of design technology in a number of ways as they engage in exploration and investigation. In an open-ended, play-based setting, children may explore this area through construction with wooden blocks, junk modelling, den building, building with bricks, and using simple tools such as hammers, saws and hand drills. They might explore ways of joining materials using sellotape, masking tape, glue, treasury tags and hole punches, and string. They might explore shaping and moulding using playdough, bread dough, quick-dry clay and wet sand.

All of the previously mentioned tasks offer opportunities for children to develop important fine motor skills – the ability to move small muscles that control movements in our hands and fingers. Fine motor skills also include movements of the lips, tongue and eyes. Fine motor skills are essential for children to master tasks such as zipping up a coat, using a knife and fork, and later, using a pencil to write. Gross motor skills support the bigger movements a child makes, such as running, hopping, climbing, skipping, jumping, and it is on this foundation that children then develop the fine motor skills needed to manipulate smaller objects. Design technology offers many opportunities for children to develop fine motor skills and as teachers we should plan for this.

If you are teaching DT in Key Stage 1, it would be helpful to find out about some of the opportunities to explore and create with materials that children had in the early years. This will help you to build upon the foundations that were laid and to continue to support children's progress.

At the end of reception, children at the expected level of development will have achieved what is set out in the Early Learning Goal, Expressive Arts and Design: Creating with Materials.

Children at the expected level of development will:

- safely use and explore a variety of materials, tools and techniques, experimenting with colour, design, texture, form and function
- share their creations, explaining the process they have used
- make use of props and materials when role playing characters in narratives and stories. (DfE, 2022b)

Using tools, constructing, making and exploring all contribute to a young child's ability to make sense of the made world around them.

Key Elements of the Design Technology Curriculum

Design technology is an innovative subject in primary school where children solve real-world problems through the process of design. There are three main elements of this subject for us to consider: construction, textiles and cooking.

When we approach our DT curriculum, we need to think about how we deliver these elements in a structured way so that children can make progress over time:

- What are the steps a child needs to take to get better at construction?
- What do I need to model to support children's understanding of stitching and fixing techniques?
- How do I create a nutritious recipe?

The National Curriculum divides design technology into Key Stage 1 (Years 1 and 2) and Key Stage 2 (Years 3–6). There are two main sections: the first is designing and making, and the second is cooking and nutrition.

In Key Stage 1, the DT curriculum is outlined as follows:

Design

- design purposeful, functional, appealing products for themselves and other users based on design criteria
- generate, develop, model and communicate their ideas through talking, drawing, templates, mock-ups and, where appropriate, information and communication technology.

Make

- select from and use a range of tools and equipment to perform practical tasks (for example, cutting, shaping, joining and finishing)
- select from and use a wide range of materials and components, including construction materials, textiles and ingredients, according to their characteristics.

Evaluate

- explore and evaluate a range of existing products
- evaluate their ideas and products against design criteria.

Technical knowledge

- build structures, exploring how they can be made stronger, stiffer and more stable

- explore and use mechanisms (for example, levers, sliders, wheels and axles) in their products.

In Key Stage 2, the curriculum outlines the following:
Design

- use research and develop design criteria to inform the design of innovative, functional, appealing products that are fit for purpose, aimed at particular individuals or groups
- generate, develop, model and communicate their ideas through discussion, annotated sketches, cross-sectional and exploded diagrams, prototypes, pattern pieces and computer-aided design.

Make

- select from and use a wide range of tools and equipment to perform practical tasks (for example, cutting, shaping, joining and finishing) accurately
- select from and use a wide range of materials and components, including construction materials, textiles and ingredients, according to their functional properties and aesthetic qualities.

Evaluate

- investigate and analyse a range of existing products
- evaluate their ideas and products against their own design criteria and consider the views of others to improve their work
- understand how key events and individuals in design and technology have helped shape the world.

Technical knowledge

- apply their understanding of how to strengthen, stiffen and reinforce more complex structures
- understand and use mechanical systems in their products (for example, gears, pulleys, cams, levers and linkages)
- understand and use electrical systems in their products (for example, series circuits incorporating switches, bulbs, buzzers and motors)
- apply their understanding of computing to programme, monitor and control their products. (DfE, 2013a)

The second important element of the design technology curriculum is cooking and nutrition. This is included in the National Curriculum at primary level to support pupils' knowledge and understanding of feeding themselves and others, both affordably and nutritiously. Cooking is also more than just a life-sustaining skill; it is an expression of creativity, of culture and brings people together. The National Curriculum (DfE, 2013a) divides this content into key stages as follows:

Key Stage 1

- use the basic principles of a healthy and varied diet to prepare dishes
- understand where food comes from.

Key Stage 2

- understand and apply the principles of a healthy and varied diet
- prepare and cook a variety of predominantly savoury dishes, using a range of cooking techniques
- understand seasonality, and know where and how a variety of ingredients are grown, reared, caught and processed.

Schools assign these elements of design technology to specific year groups and decide how to allocate curriculum time to each area of study. As previously mentioned, cooking and nutrition is frequently blocked to allow children time to plan and make their recipes.

Within a unit of design technology, it is important we think about the sequence of the taught content, how we are building upon what children have already learned and created, and how we are moving their learning on; introducing them to new knowledge and skills.

If you are on a placement or begin your career in a free school or an academy, the institution may have chosen to use its curriculum freedoms to create a design technology curriculum that does not follow the National Curriculum. In this case, you may want to look at the curriculum you have and explore the following:

- How is design technology introduced in the early years and Key Stage 1?
- How does the curriculum develop skills over time? For example, when do children learn about cooking, what do they make and what skills do they develop over time?
- Which significant designers do children learn about through the curriculum?

How Do You Build Subject Knowledge?

The design technology subject knowledge is vast – from cooking to construction to textiles and sewing. As primary teachers, we need to know a range of techniques, mechanisms, tools and design processes. In each of the areas covered by the National Curriculum in DT, we must have the specialised *content knowledge* required to teach the subject well, without, as we have mentioned, being specialists ourselves. We also need *pedagogical knowledge* – knowledge of how we teach design technology in our primary classrooms.

It is our responsibility to recognise our own knowledge gaps and to fill them by reading, researching and practising our own skills. If we don't know how to draw a cross-sectional diagram, this is something we need to learn. If we don't know how a pulley works, we need to find out. The journey of our own learning will be ongoing throughout our teaching career, but at this early stage whilst training, it is important to identify areas that we need to focus on. The National Curriculum outlines content we need to teach, but as we have said before, it won't teach you what you need to know in order to do this. Seek advice from subject leaders where possible, and if you can, arrange to watch them teach design technology. Look for how experienced teachers organise their resources, how they explain and model, and how they structure their design technology lessons. Make use of resources such as subject associations and museums who often have an education arm to support teachers. The subject knowledge audit in the appendix of this book will help you to focus in on your own knowledge and to identify areas to work on.

Whilst we are developing our own subject knowledge, we must also consider pedagogical knowledge. This is concerned with the 'how' of teaching design technology to primary children. When we've secured *what* we want children to focus their design skills on, we need to think about *how* we will teach them. We need to guide children through the design process, from the research and development stage, through the making of their product to the evaluation stage. There will be elements we need to model carefully, perhaps using a visualiser, for example teaching children how to use a pattern piece when working with textiles. There will be occasions when we need to give children time and space to practise: threading needles, chopping vegetables with a knife, cutting out a pattern. There will also be occasions when a design element fails: glue doesn't set as expected, a cake burns in the oven, a mechanism jams. We must support children to work through these challenges and view them as essential parts of the learning and design process.

Some pedagogical points to consider for design technology:

- What measures can I take to ensure children are working safely in my design technology lessons?
- How will I check on children's prior learning? (What have they made in previous years? What tools have they used? Have they learned about the design, make, evaluate process before?)
- How will I explicitly teach the key vocabulary needed? For example, oral rehearsal, discussing etymology, looking for other words that are linked to the key word, identifying roots of words, putting key words in a sentence.
- Once we have established a purpose for our design, how will I break the process down into small, manageable chunks, ensuring children are not overloaded? What am I saying? What am I modelling for the children? Are they listening, copying, exploring, expressing, working independently, and is that what I want them to do?
- Which materials and mechanical systems will children have an opportunity to use and explore? For example, card, paper, wood, textiles, plastics, electronics, gears, pulleys, wheels.

- Which ingredients will we use for cooking? Which are affordable, easy to source, nutritious?

Summary

What we have discussed in this chapter:

- Primary design technology asks children to solve real-world problems with creative solutions.
- A high-quality design technology curriculum is well sequenced and clearly identifies what the children will design from EYFS to Key Stage 2. This clarity helps teachers to teach effective lessons and helps children to learn, remember and be able to do more over time.
- Our own knowledge of both design technology subject content (what we teach) and pedagogy (how we teach) is crucial and will develop throughout our teaching career.

Signposts to Additional Resources

Exploring these resources will deepen your understanding of the role of design technology in the primary curriculum:

- The Consortium of Local Education Authorities for the Provision of Science Services – https://primary.cleapss.org.uk
- The Design and Technology Association – www.data.org.uk
- The National Society for Education in Art and Design – www.nsead.org

---

QUESTIONS TO ASK EXPERTS

The Initial Teacher Training Core Content Framework (DfE, 2019a) specifies that during your training you need to have input from experts. Here are some design technology curriculum questions you could ask when you have the chance:

- Can you help me to understand how the design technology curriculum is structured?
- What materials are available to help me prepare my design technology lessons?
- Which designers will children learn about in the key stage I am working in?
- What do we expect children in the year I am working in to be able to do in design technology?

Discussion Questions

1 In small groups, read the Early Learning Goals for Expressive Arts and Design. Discuss what our youngest children might make and design in early years.
2 In small groups, read the National Curriculum for design technology in Key Stage 1 and Key Stage 2. How do knowledge and skills build over time?
3 How can we help our pupils to develop their design skills over time?
4 Which areas of design technology do you want to learn more about to secure your subject knowledge? How will you do this, and what resources will you use?

14

PE

Why Teach PE to Primary Children?

The Parliament Post (2021) shared concerning data that 35% of children are overweight or obese by the time they leave primary school. As a nation, we have a duty to try and reverse this trend as a matter of urgency and we – as educators – can play a key role through our PE curriculum. Not only does teaching PE support our children to live a healthier physical lifestyle, but we can also find many other benefits to teaching this subject:

- By developing gross and fine motor skills, particularly in the early years, we help pupils' wider skills such as handwriting and balancing so they can enjoy a successful future.
- It builds opportunities for children to both compete and collaborate with each other and this supports them in developing healthy relationships.
- By laying the foundation to living a healthy lifestyle at a young age we can prevent the development of more serious medical conditions later in life.

- There is strong evidence of the link between an active lifestyle and positive mental health.
- It provides opportunities for all children to learn how to swim which is an important life-saving skill.

Whilst there is much evidence of the benefits of living an active lifestyle, the Youth Sport Trust (2021) has noted that children have become more sedentary since the Covid-19 pandemic and are only spending, on average, 30 minutes of their day on being active. Therefore, we must make sure children are receiving great PE teaching in school, so that we provide them with the foundations of living a healthy lifestyle.

Ofsted (2022a) published its subject review of PE which is a useful document to guide us in what the research suggests good teaching in PE looks like. As with all of Ofsted's subject reviews, they are large documents and we always recommend you read the full detail to understand what is most relevant to your context. However, some of what we feel is most relevant to primary teaching is summarised below:

- A good PE curriculum will carefully consider what it wants pupils to be able to do and know more of. Time should be built into the curriculum so that children revisit and deepen their knowledge. Feedback should be provided which focuses on how to improve.
- The early years curriculum provides children with a strong foundation for being successful in PE and it is important that the curriculum considers EYFS and how the KS1 curriculum builds upon what children have learnt before.
- PE should not just focus on movement; it should also develop children's knowledge of strategies and rules.
- PE should be inclusive for all pupils. It is essential that schools ensure all pupils can fully participate and feel successful.
- Opportunities for competition should be threaded through the curriculum and pupils should have the knowledge required to participate in competition meaningfully.

The research above provides us with key aspects to consider when designing and teaching our PE curriculum, but we can sometimes be led by our own interests or what we are most comfortable with when we teach PE. For example, if we have a particular interest in netball, we may want to teach this sport each time we teach the games aspect of PE as we know the rules and strategies and therefore will have more confidence delivering this sport. However, just like every other subject in the curriculum, it needs to be carefully sequenced and, as the research above suggests, there must be clarity around what we teach and when to ensure there are opportunities for pupils to revisit learning and become better.

If we allowed all teachers to choose what they wanted to teach in PE, it might be true that children would get exposed to different sports, but they would not be able to develop the skills and knowledge of a particular sport in a meaningful manner, and most would not have a high rate of success as they would not have the opportunity to practise and embed what they have learnt. If we want the children we teach to feel successful in PE, we must provide ample opportunity for them to develop a deep understanding of the different aspects of the PE curriculum so that they can have high levels of success and develop a love of PE. Therefore, one of the careful decisions curriculum leaders need to make is what content they choose to teach and how this will be carefully sequenced. Whilst it can be tempting to include a lot of different content in the PE curriculum – teaching a great variety of sports/dance/athletics etc. – we should instead deliberately choose content the children will benefit from most. Planning opportunities to revisit and build upon prior learning in these aspects will result in higher levels of success. Whilst you may have a passion for a specific sport or activity, such as dance or gymnastics, which does not form part of your school's curriculum, you could still share this with the children via extracurricular clubs, however our own interests should not be a barrier to a sequenced curriculum.

As we mentioned earlier in Chapter 4 on diversity, PE also provides us with an important opportunity to challenge some stereotypes that may exist. For example, if there are specific sports which are more typically associated with the success of a particular gender, we can show the children role models for this sport from the opposite gender. Equally, we can find much inspiration in our Paralympians to show how these individuals overcame great odds to be such a success in their field.

How Is PE Subject Knowledge Sequenced?

The primary National Curriculum for PE has four aims, which are to ensure pupils:

- develop the competence to excel in a broad range of physical activities
- are physically active for sustained periods of time
- engage in competitive sports and activities
- lead a healthy, active lifestyle.

For the primary curriculum, these aims are further set out in the subject content for Key Stages 1 (KS1) and 2 (KS2). The subject content includes a brief introduction, three bullet points for KS1, six bullet points for KS2, and a section on swimming and water safety. We will discuss the key elements of the curriculum later in this chapter, but our first job as teachers is to sequence this content into small steps so that children can achieve the end of key stage content. As pupils work through the sequenced curriculum, we want them to be building their knowledge and making progress towards achieving the four key aims outlined above.

When we think about knowledge in PE, it can be helpful to think about it in two forms: substantive knowledge and disciplinary knowledge. Substantive knowledge is the essence of PE. It considers the facts of this subject and imparts key aspects such as the different types of defence in different sports, or how dribbling in basketball is different to dribbling in hockey. Disciplinary knowledge is knowing how the knowledge we have in PE has been constructed or revealed. How do attackers in certain sports become so skilled? What steps might a gymnast take to improve their technique? Questions such as these help children to develop disciplinary understanding in PE.

Although there may not be a consensus on what sports we should teach children or how much time a school should dedicate to teaching PE, we must still consider what we will be teaching our children and how we will break this down into small, manageable steps.

Let us now look at an example for a Key Stage 1 unit in PE.

What Do I Want My Children to Know and Be Able to Do at the End of This Unit?

The Key Stage 1 curriculum requires children to participate in team games and to be able to defend and attack. It also requires children to be able to throw and catch effectively. I therefore need my children to participate successfully in a team game (I will choose basketball), which will also require them to throw, catch, defend and attack. For the purpose of this planning, I will consider how I might plan this in Year 1 with an awareness of the sport.

Where Will I Start?

I will think about what they already know and this will require me to look back at the curriculum to see what the children have already studied in PE. Some questions I might consider are:

- What have the children learnt in EYFS which can help them learn this sequence?
- How will I check they have retained this knowledge?
- What does the ELG data tell me about my class, and will they need support with fine or gross motor skills?
- What support do I need to have in place for those children who might struggle to access the learning?

Once I have clarified the above, I will then consider what I want the children to achieve by the time I have taught this unit – in this instance, I want them to understand how to defend, attack, become better at throwing and catching, and participate in a team game (basketball). I now need to think of the different small steps I will plan for the sequence of learning in order to support the children to be successful.

What Will My Sequence of Learning Look Like?

Step 1: Prior learning – set tasks to check children have remembered and can do what they have been previously taught so I can build upon this

Step 2: Dribbling basketball – hand–eye coordination

Step 3: Throwing with a focus on passing

Step 4: Throwing with a focus on attacking and defending

Step 5: Dribbling and shooting

Step 6: Playing a competitive game of basketball.

Whilst the above is mapped out across six steps, this could be across more/fewer lessons. For example, I may realise that children need further feedback and practice of dribbling, so it would be necessary for me to do two or three lessons on this aspect to help children to get better at dribbling as this is essential for future lessons.

What Does Progress Look Like Within This Unit?

Progress in PE will be mainly through what you can see in your lessons as a teacher. You will see the children getting better at dribbling, throwing, and so on, and this will inform you of the progress they are making and of what you need to do next to further support them.

Within this unit, progress might look like the following:

- Is their understanding of vocabulary improving in PE? For example, are they using vocabulary such as defence, attack, dribbling? This is vocabulary children will use across a range of different sports, so you may wish to deliberately plan opportunities for other sports which use the term 'dribbling', such as hockey and football, as this will further deepen their understanding.
- Are children getting physically better at throwing, catching, dribbling, and so on? Are you noticing that due to lots of deliberate practice they are becoming more fluent with these skills?
- Are children progressing with their understanding of more generic elements of sport, such as the rules of games and competition? For example, whilst teaching dribbling you might explain how basketballers dribble and the rules for this – you then may see the children applying this knowledge when they are playing the competitive game. Additionally, you may notice that children are responding more positively when they lose, or are showing more resilience when a skill is tricky; this is all evidence of progress too.

Do remember that this sequence of lessons is one part of a much bigger curriculum. Children will revisit this sport again later in the year in Year 2 and develop on what they have learnt in this unit. For example, next steps might be dribbling with greater speed or throwing with greater focus on a target – this all helps the children to increase their mastery and become better by the time they leave primary school.

Early Years

In the early years, the subject of PE does not appear as PE but instead it is referred to as Physical Development, and is an extremely important educational programme within the EYFS, so much so that it is one of the areas a child must achieve the Early Learning Goal (ELG) in to be considered as achieving an overall good level of development (if a child achieves the ELG in the prime areas of literacy and maths, they are considered to have achieved a good overall level of development). Physical Development within the EYFS framework considers both fine and gross motor skills, and for a child to achieve the expected level within these areas, they will need to have achieved the ELG content outlined below:

ELG: Gross Motor Skills – children at the expected level of development will:

- negotiate space and obstacles safely, with consideration for themselves and others
- demonstrate strength, balance and coordination when playing
- move energetically, such as running, jumping, dancing, hopping, skipping and climbing.

ELG: Fine Motor Skills – children at the expected level of development will:

- hold a pencil effectively in preparation for fluent writing – using the tripod grip in almost all cases
- use a range of small tools, including scissors, paintbrushes and cutlery
- begin to show accuracy and care when drawing.

It is important that we are aware of those children who have achieved the ELGs outlined above as this will help us identify what children know and what our curriculum in KS1 should be building upon. It will also help us to identify those children who may need additional support.

Key Elements of the PE Curriculum

The KS1 and KS2 curriculum should build upon what the children have already achieved by the end of the reception year. We have already outlined the four aims of the curriculum above and established that there is not a huge amount of content to the statutory framework for PE, but there are some key elements we need to know as practitioners.

The subject content for KS1 states: Pupils should develop fundamental movement skills, become increasingly competent and confident and access a broad range of opportunities to extend their agility, balance and coordination, individually and with others. They should be able to engage in competitive (both against self and against others) and co-operative physical activities, in a range of increasingly challenging situations.

Pupils should be taught to:

- master basic movements including running, jumping, throwing and catching, as well as developing balance, agility and coordination, and begin to apply these in a range of activities
- participate in team games, developing simple tactics for attacking and defending
- perform dances using simple movement patterns. (DfE, 2013a)

The subject content for KS2 states: Pupils should continue to apply and develop a broader range of skills, learning how to use them in different ways and to link them to make actions and sequences of movement. They should enjoy communicating, collaborating and competing with each other. They should develop an understanding of how to improve in different physical activities and sports, and learn how to evaluate and recognise their own success.

Pupils should be taught to:

- use running, jumping, throwing and catching in isolation and in combination, play competitive games, modified where appropriate (for example, badminton, basketball, cricket, football, hockey, netball, rounders and tennis), and apply basic principles suitable for attacking and defending
- develop flexibility, strength, technique, control and balance (for example, through athletics and gymnastics), and perform dances using a range of movement patterns
- take part in outdoor and adventurous activity challenges both individually and within a team
- compare their performances with previous ones and demonstrate improvement to achieve their personal best. (DfE, 2013a)

In addition to the above, there is also a requirement to teach swimming and water safety.

All schools must provide swimming instruction either in Key Stage 1 or Key Stage 2. In particular, pupils should be taught to:

- swim competently, confidently and proficiently over a distance of at least 25 metres
- use a range of strokes effectively (for example, front crawl, backstroke and breaststroke)
- perform safe self-rescue in different water-based situations. (DfE, 2013a)

The theme of 'movement' is threaded throughout the curriculum. In KS1, children will explore and become more experienced in a range of movements such as throwing, catching, jumping, balancing and coordination. Children should get plenty of opportunity and feedback to improve and master these movements. As they enter KS2, children will build upon these movements and think about how they can combine them and use them more strategically in a range of sports, dance or in the field of gymnastics. It is important that we enable pupils to master these skills in KS1 as, without this, they will struggle to access the KS2 curriculum.

Children should be participating in a range of team games in KS1 and this progresses to competitive team games in KS2. As previously mentioned, it is important that children revisit the same games so that they can master and build upon previous learning. This will enable them to be more successful when playing these games competitively. The curriculum also requires us to build children's knowledge of the rules of these games; again, we can build this gradually throughout the course of the curriculum by re-visiting and building upon the prior learning as well as making links with other sports they may have played. For example, if they have previously played basketball and understood the term 'dribbling', we could revisit this term and consider how this might apply to a sport like hockey. The same is true when we talk about defenders and attackers in sports – by introducing this knowledge and appropriate vocabulary to children in KS1, they can apply and build upon this knowledge as they enter KS2.

In KS2, pupils are required to take part in outdoor adventurous activities. This is an aspect of the curriculum which not all schools teach well, or they often link it to a school trip in Year 6. Whilst it can be acceptable for the outdoor adventurous learning to happen as part of a trip, there would be some questions you would need to carefully consider, such as: Do all children attend the school trip? If not, how do they access this aspect of the school trip? If this is just a one-off experience, how do children build upon prior knowledge? Do they have enough time to practise and embed new knowledge? It is better if the outdoor adventurous activity is threaded through the curriculum like all other aspects of PE, so that pupils encounter it year on year and can build upon prior learning. Examples include bouldering, hiking and orienteering. There is often a specialist level of expertise required for these activities so schools may source external providers to teach these aspects of the curriculum.

Another requirement of the National Curriculum is that we teach swimming and water safety. This is an incredibly important aspect of the curriculum that we must not overlook. We know that children from more affluent families are much more likely to be able to swim than those from disadvantaged backgrounds, so it is essential we close this gap in swimming. Few schools have their own swimming pool, so it is not unusual for certain year groups to attend the local swimming pool to access their curriculum lessons for swimming. Whilst some schools may outsource this to external swimming instructors, we still need to have an overview of the curriculum the children are being taught and how well they are progressing through it. There is a requirement for all schools to publish on their website how many children can swim 25 metres so we do need to know this information and have a plan in place for those who are not achieving this target. If your school outsources swimming tuition, some questions you will want to consider are: How is the swimming curriculum sequenced? How often do children swim? What support is put in place for those pupils struggling to swim? How is self-rescue taught?

A final comment we will make is the importance of time in PE lessons. In PE, we will face different challenges as we are not operating within the typical classroom – we will be bringing children outside the classroom to a pitch, playground, PE hall, and so on, and this requires specific planning. We need to use every minute of our PE lessons wisely and ensure no time is wasted. This means that we need to have clear routines and expectations:

- How will you ensure pupils get changed into their PE kit quickly? Often, time can be wasted because children spend too much time getting ready for their PE lesson. Strategies like making it a competition against the clock can be a fun way to ensure children get ready in the shortest amount of time possible. Your school may consider letting children attend in their PE kits on their PE day to ensure maximum time is spent in the lesson.
- What plan do you have for children who forget their PE kit or who have inappropriate PE kit? Some schools have spare PE kit for children if they require this. It is worth asking children first thing in the morning whether they have their PE kit so you can deal with any missing kit before the lesson and ensure little time is wasted.
- If your lesson requires resources, consider how these can be set up before the lesson. Is there an additional adult who can assist with this? Can you train the children to help hand out resources quickly, so you can maximise the time in your lesson?
- Does your lesson involve team elements? If so, choose the teams before the lesson yourself. This will save time, but, more importantly, it will mean you can differentiate your lessons so the teams are equal and you will be able to target your feedback effectively. If you let children choose the teams themselves, they may choose their friends first and you have a higher risk of uneven teams which will make it difficult for all children to be successful and motivated.

As you can see from the above, the statutory elements of the PE curriculum are very broad and the National Curriculum document itself does not offer much detail around the small steps we should teach in order to support children to achieve the end of key stage expectations. It is, therefore, the responsibility of individual schools to carefully build their curriculum so that children are able to achieve the expectations set out by the National Curriculum.

How Do You Build Subject Knowledge?

How do you feel when you think about teaching PE? Is it a subject you really enjoyed in school? A subject you studied for your A Levels or even at university? Or is it a subject which makes you nervous? A subject you did not enjoy so much at school? Regardless of your personal experience of PE, we all need to be able to teach it well and to inspire a love of the subject.

We will all have different starting points with our subject knowledge in PE. You may have a particularly strong knowledge of a specific aspect of the PE curriculum, such as swimming or dance, and therefore will need to reflect upon the different aspects of the curriculum as a starting point for building your knowledge.

As with all subjects, the best place to start when assessing your subject knowledge is with the content of the National Curriculum. By reading what the curriculum outlines and reflecting honestly on the different aspects, it will provide you with a baseline. You will not be able to learn and know everything at once, so if you are in a particular key stage we advise that you start with this. The subject knowledge audit in the appendix of this book will support you in focusing your own areas for development. When we show a genuine interest in a subject, we can help build our knowledge so watch expert teachers teach PE; read blogs; do your own research and practise the content of the curriculum yourself so that you build up your own confidence.

As well as having secure knowledge of the content of the curriculum, it is important that we have secure pedagogical knowledge around how best to teach PE. All subjects are unique, and some pedagogical approaches will look different in PE compared to maths, for example. Whilst we cannot cover all aspects of pedagogical knowledge in PE, here are some points to consider:

- How will you reconnect with prior learning? With PE, this might be practical – do you know the previous movements children have been taught? Do you know what simple movement patterns they were taught in KS1?
- Modelling in PE will often require expert demonstrations – this means you will need to have a broad knowledge to model clearly for the children. For example, you will need to be able to model how to hold a hockey stick; perform a dance movement; serve a tennis ball; and possibly even swim a backstroke. This may sound daunting, but do not worry as there are many solutions for support with modelling. You can make use of video footage of experts modelling different aspects of PE for children to analyse and you can guide their thinking – for example, you could watch footage of a gymnast, pause the video and direct attention to the most important aspect which you want the children to replicate. If you are making use of IT, consider what space you will use to share this if your lesson is outdoors or the PE hall does

not have IT facilities (you may show this in the classroom first). If there is anything you are unclear about, remember to speak to your school's PE lead for advice.

- You will need to ensure you have a secure understanding of vocabulary in the PE curriculum and how you will teach this (e.g. opponent, agility, attack and defend). There will also be specific vocabulary which relates to the type of dance or sport your school chooses to teach.
- PE is very resource heavy and you need to have secure knowledge when it comes to using the wide range of different resources – from climbing equipment to javelins.
- Finally, something which makes PE unique is the importance of health and safety in this subject. You may be required to have an overview of the risk assessment for the swimming pool or consider carefully how to make outdoor adventurous sports as safe as possible. PE needs to be taught safely and, as teachers, it is our duty to ensure this happens. Speak to the relevant member of staff responsible for health and safety to learn more about your school's expectations.

Summary

What we have discussed in this chapter:

- There are many benefits to teaching PE to our children.
- A high-quality PE curriculum needs to be well sequenced. We should provide children with the opportunity to learn fewer sports really well so they have a better chance of being successful and developing a love of PE.
- The PE curriculum is broad and requires a teacher to have an in-depth understanding of both the content and pedagogical knowledge required.

Signposts to Additional Resources

There is a wide variety of resources available to support you to teach PE, but a selection of some high-quality ones we recommend include:

- Association for Physical Education (AFPE) has a range of useful information to help you become better at teaching PE – www.afpe.org.uk/physical-education
- Primary Physical Education Assembly – www.ppea.org.uk
- Youth Sport Trust – www.youthsporttrust.org/primary-pe-activities

━━━━━━━ QUESTIONS TO ASK EXPERTS ━━━━━━━

The Initial Teaching Training Core Content Framework (DfE, 2019a) specifies that during your training you need to have input from experts. Here are some PE curriculum questions you could ask the PE lead in your school:

- How has the PE curriculum been organised from EYFS to Year 6? Why?
- Does the school use a scheme for teaching PE? What is the justification for this?
- What sports will children learn about? Do they revisit this sport numerous times or just once?
- My subject knowledge in X is not secure – how could I develop this?
- How is swimming taught in this school?
- What outdoor adventurous activity do the children learn?

Discussion Questions

1 In small groups, look at the aims of the PE curriculum. Discuss whether you think these are reasonable for children to learn in KS1 and KS2.
2 In small groups, look at the Physical Development section of the early years framework. Discuss what our youngest children will learn in EYFS to get them ready for KS1 PE.
3 What aspect of PE are you most/least confident to teach? How can you develop your knowledge of this?
4 A PE curriculum is at the heart of a child growing up to be physically and mentally healthy. Discuss this statement.

15

LANGUAGES

Why Teach Languages to Primary Children?

Speaking more than one language opens doors – it brings us to another culture and way of life. When we inspire children to love and become curious about a second language, it provides a foundation they can build upon when they enter secondary school. We want our pupils to develop their cultural capital and have an awareness of life beyond their own country – a rich language curriculum provides this.

The National Curriculum only requires us to teach languages to KS2 (not KS1 or EYFS) and schools can choose either a modern foreign language of their choice or an ancient foreign language. Even though it has been a requirement for primary schools to teach a language since 2014 and schools have autonomy to choose the language they wish to study, some schools have taken longer to implement this aspect of the curriculum as some unique challenges can be a barrier to the teaching of languages:

- Some primary schools might not have an expert in the language they are teaching. This can make it difficult for teachers to feel confident teaching and can result in schools changing their curriculum approach (e.g. changing language choice).
- It can be difficult to find quality professional development for primary practitioners. Whilst other subjects have support through hubs (e.g. maths and computing), languages does not currently have this support in place. As schools often study a range of languages, it can be difficult to find the right development for the languages your school teaches.
- If the curriculum continuously changes, it can mean children do not get the opportunity to learn the language in a logical and sequential manner, so that they finish KS2 without the foundations required for KS3.

If we want our children to have a real opportunity to gain curiosity about and a love for the language we teach them, we must ensure that our subject knowledge is secure; have a sequenced curriculum which enables children to get better at their language; and ensure we dedicate sufficient time in our timetable to the teaching of that language.

Ofsted's research review of languages (Ofsted, 2021c) provides us with some of the features a high-quality language curriculum may have, such as those given below which are relevant to primary teaching:

- Learning in the classroom is not left to chance and is deliberately planned.
- When teaching a target language, teachers carefully plan this and provide pupils with opportunities to practise.
- Teachers are explicit when correcting errors.
- Phonics is well planned for in the language.
- Vocabulary development is carefully planned for.
- Grammar is planned for sequentially and teachers think carefully about what children need to learn first and then build upon this.

How Is Language Subject Knowledge Sequenced?

Sequencing subject knowledge in language simply means considering the order in which we teach language content. As is outlined below in the section on elements of the primary curriculum, the KS2 content of study for languages provides us with the content we need children to know by the end of KS2 – this content is not set out year by year and it is up to the individual school how it plans this content. Some schools may opt to purchase a ready-made scheme for the language they have chosen, but teachers still need to ensure the content is sequenced appropriately; that the tasks set out in the scheme do not distract from the intended learning; and that it is as ambitious as the content set out in the National Curriculum. Just as per Chapter 5 on early reading, it is essential that the curriculum carefully plans the phonetic elements of the language being taught – as teachers, we should be fully aware of what sounds are being taught and when, so we can use this information to deliberately plan the vocabulary we will be teaching in our lessons. Phonics needs to be systematic.

We need to avoid a 'shopping list' approach to the teaching of languages in the primary curriculum. This is where we just choose a range of activities or experiences to teach the children, instead of thinking about content in small steps which build upon prior learning. For instance, when we look at the curriculum, we need to teach some of the below:

- songs and rhymes
- familiar words and phrases
- descriptions of places
- basic grammar.

Using the shopping list approach, we might just choose a different place each year and teach the children some familiar words to describe this place. Whilst this would technically be teaching the above, if lessons are not deliberately planned to build upon what children have already learnt, they would not support children's long-term retention of the learning. In the case of songs and rhymes, children could choose and sing different rhymes each year but we should plan out the rhymes taught in each year so that they can become progressively more challenging and build upon existing learning.

Let's explore how one of the KS2 requirements might be sequenced. At the end of KS2, children should be able to describe people, places, things and actions orally and in writing, so let's consider what this might look like.

Where Will I Start?

The statement above provides me with the end point – this is what I want children to know by the time they finish Year 6. I need to think about how I will sequentially build knowledge over time so that the children can achieve this. You may want to ask yourself the following:

- Whilst children might first be learning this language in Year 3, how can I still connect to their existing learning? For example, they know the word adjective from English lessons so I can use this knowledge.
- I need to start with simple and familiar descriptions to begin with and then build upon this in Years 4, 5 and 6. What can I get children to describe over

time so they can connect with prior knowledge? What descriptive vocabulary can I teach children which they can use in a number of different contexts?

- What can I do to support children in my class who have not yet secured an understanding of the past, present and future?

What Will My Sequence of Learning Look Like (Across KS2)?

There are numerous ways we could plan this across KS2, but here is just one example:

Step 1: An introduction to simple nouns within the classroom that children are familiar with. I will deliberately plan this vocabulary and provide opportunities to practise. The vocabulary I use should be linked to how phonics is sequenced within the curriculum so that children's progress is not being hindered by a lack of phonetic knowledge – this aspect should be considered at all steps.

Step 2: I will provide descriptive words which will support children's ability to describe the nouns. Children will focus on rehearsing these simple descriptions orally. I may introduce some opportunities to write down the key words.

Step 3: I will extend children's knowledge of nouns and adjectives, continuing to use familiar contexts. For example, I will focus on them and describing their appearance. Children will also use conversation to discuss what they like and dislike. I will reconnect with the prior knowledge they have learnt and provide more opportunities to practise. They will rehearse this orally and write a simple sentence.

Step 4: I will now extend opportunities for description beyond themselves and common nouns and extend this to describing other familiar, but more challenging contexts such as the city or local area. I will reconnect with the previous vocabulary they have learnt and model how they can use this. For example, if they are describing the local area I will reconnect with their colour knowledge. They will also reconnect with what they like and dislike and use this vocabulary when describing the local area. They will write a few sentences describing this context.

Step 5: I will continue to teach children specific descriptive vocabulary, again linking and extending the prior knowledge they have. For example, I may choose a setting in a local area such as a café and teach descriptive language and introduce conversational aspects to develop oral language.

*As these steps are across a key stage, each step would be broken down into smaller steps so that children can learn and practise the small components used.

What Does Progress Look Like?

There will be two key indicators of progress – pupils' vocabulary and pupils' writing:

- Are children using the specific vocabulary taught? As children progress through the lesson content, they are continuously building upon their vocabulary knowledge. As I have deliberately planned the words I want the children to know and use, I will be listening out for these words when children are practising orally, and I will also check whether these words are being used in their writing. I will not only be listening out for the use of the words, but I will also want to see progress in the accuracy of pronunciation and precision of use. Key to this will be linking the vocabulary I teach with the phonetic knowledge they have been taught.
- Progress will also be evident in writing over time. In the beginning lessons, the children may be writing just some key words and phrases but by the time they leave KS2, they should be writing a few sentences. There will also be progress evident in the quality of sentences written by the children – are spellings accurate? Is grammatical knowledge more refined? Are children more confident in writing from memory?

Elements of the Languages' Curriculum

Since September 2014, the teaching of a modern or an ancient language in primary school has become statutory. The National Curriculum does not tell schools what language they should teach or how much time they should dedicate to the teaching of that language; these decisions are made at school level and each school will have a different approach.

As mentioned earlier, the curriculum for languages is only set out for KS2. This does not mean that some schools do not teach it in KS1 or EYFS, but this is a school decision and the content for those lessons will be decided at school level. As a trainee teacher and when ensuring we are meeting the statutory requirements of the National Curriculum, we only need to focus on the content outlined for KS2.

There are four aims for schools to achieve by the end of KS2. Children should:

- understand and respond to spoken and written language from a variety of authentic sources
- speak with increasing confidence, fluency and spontaneity, finding ways of communicating what they want to say, including through discussion and asking questions, and continually improving the accuracy of their pronunciation and intonation

- write at varying length, for different purposes and audiences, using the variety of grammatical structures that they have learnt
- discover and develop an appreciation of a range of writing in the language studied.

In addition to the four aims above, the curriculum content is set out in 12 bullet points. This provides the content children should have been taught by the time they leave Year 6, and schools will need to consider how the curriculum can be planned in a logical manner and when children will learn this content across KS2.
Pupils should be taught to:

- listen attentively to spoken language and show understanding by joining in and responding
- explore the patterns and sounds of language through songs and rhymes and link the spelling, sound and meaning of words
- engage in conversations; ask and answer questions; express opinions and respond to those of others; seek clarification and help*
- speak in sentences, using familiar vocabulary, phrases and basic language structures
- develop accurate pronunciation and intonation so that others understand when they are reading aloud or using familiar words and phrases*
- present ideas and information orally to a range of audiences*
- read carefully and show understanding of words, phrases and simple writing
- appreciate stories, songs, poems and rhymes in the language
- broaden their vocabulary and develop their ability to understand new words that are introduced into familiar written material, including through using a dictionary
- write phrases from memory, and adapt these to create new sentences, to express ideas clearly
- describe people, places, things and actions orally* and in writing
- understand basic grammar appropriate to the language being studied, including (where relevant): feminine, masculine and neuter forms and the conjugation of high-frequency verbs; key features and patterns of the language; how to apply these, for instance, to build sentences; and how these differ from or are similar to English.

The starred (*) content above will not be applicable to ancient languages.

Navigating a language curriculum at primary level can be tricky – if we don't have a language expert in our school or a good command of the language we are teaching, we need to ensure that we have a thorough understanding of the subject content so we can teach it effectively.

When we approach the planning of a language unit of work, we would need to think carefully about what content children need to learn first and then build upon this so they can achieve the outcomes set above. For example, if we consider that by the end of KS2 children should be able to orally and in writing describe people, we might ask:

- What people do we want children to be able to describe by the end of KS2? What adjectives do we want them to use when they are describing them?
- What other language do we need to teach them when they are describing people? For example, we will need to teach pronouns.
- When should we teach these adjectives and pronouns? What could we teach in Year 3 and then build upon in Years 4, 5 and 6?
- I want pupils to be able to orally describe people before writing – by what point in KS2 should they be able to do this orally?
- What potential barriers might we encounter when planning and teaching these aspects of the curriculum?
- Is my own subject knowledge secure?

The National Curriculum requires children to develop their speaking, writing and listening skills of the language being taught:

- Speaking is developed through conversations, phonics knowledge, pronunciation and vocabulary development of the taught language. Any curriculum will need to have phonics clearly sequenced.
- Children get better at writing in the chosen language through developing their grammar knowledge and the expectation that they begin with writing words/ phrases and can write full sentences by the time they finish KS2.
- Listening is developed through listening to and responding appropriately through conversation, song and questions.

How Do You Build Subject Knowledge?

As we have mentioned previously, we have a responsibility to teach a wide number of subjects with a wide knowledge base, and languages are a good example of this. Linguistics tend to focus on a specific language and develop knowledge and expertise for this language. In each of the areas covered by the National Curriculum for Languages, we must have the specialised *content knowledge* required to teach the subject well, without necessarily being specialists ourselves. We also need *pedagogical knowledge* – the knowledge of how we teach language and what research tells us about best practice.

It is our responsibility to recognise our own knowledge gaps and fill them by reading, researching and informing ourselves. The journey of our own learning will be ongoing throughout our teaching career, but at this early stage whilst training, it is important to identify areas that we need to focus on. Reading the National Curriculum is an essential way to familiarise yourself with subject content, but as we have said before, it won't teach you what you need to know as a teacher.

A unique aspect of the languages' curriculum is that gaps in your subject knowledge will relate to the specific language your school teaches, and you will not know which it is until you are on placement in a school or you start your full-time teaching post. Therefore, often a good place to start is ensuring your knowledge of the grammar and syntax of language is secure and that this terminology will be transferrable. For example, your understanding of the key features and patterns of the English language will support you to compare the similarities and differences with the language being taught.

The curriculum used by your school will have resources to support that specific language and you should speak with the languages subject lead in your school who will be able to advise you on how you can effectively teach the curriculum the school has chosen. The links to the additional resources at the end of this chapter will also support you to develop your subject knowledge.

Whilst we are working on our subject knowledge, we must also consider pedagogical knowledge. This is concerned with the 'how' of teaching language. When we've secured what we want children to learn about, we need to think about *how* we will teach them. There are many different approaches to classroom pedagogy, and it is important we think deeply about what effective learning looks like in the different subjects we teach. As we have said, when you begin to look into this, you will find many debates and disagreements, and sometimes it is hard to separate opinion from fact. Often, pedagogical approaches are taken because they 'feel right', not necessarily because an evidence base has shown they are the best bet for making learning happen. Pedagogy is a huge area that cannot be covered in a meaningful way in this chapter, and we have touched on some advice from the Ofsted research into languages above. However, some other pedagogical aspects you should consider when teaching languages are:

- How will I give an opportunity to reconnect to prior learning? For example, existing vocabulary and grammatical knowledge.
- How will I explicitly teach the key vocabulary? For example, oral rehearsal, discussing etymology, looking for other words that are linked to the key word, identifying roots of words, putting key words in a sentence.
- How will I explicitly model the pronunciation of the vocabulary? Am I secure in this?
- Do I have a clear overview of the phonics the children have been taught for this language? How will I use this knowledge?

- How is grammatical knowledge developed within this lesson? Can I link this to the existing knowledge children might have from English lessons?
- Are there any misconceptions I can plan for?
- What teaching resources will I use to support children's learning? For example, sources, texts, maps, images, photographs, diagrams, videos.

Summary

What we have discussed in this chapter:

- Some of the challenges we can face as primary practitioners when teaching languages.
- The importance of having a carefully sequenced curriculum in languages and not a 'shopping list' approach.
- The languages curriculum being only statutory for KS2, though some schools may wish to teach in KS1 and EYFS.
- Deliberately planning for the teaching of vocabulary.
- That children should get better at phonics, writing, speaking and listening in the language taught.
- Each school can choose what language they teach so it is important to familiarise yourself with the language taught in your school and this will support your subject knowledge development.
- A range of resources you can use to support the teaching of languages.

Signposts to Additional Resources

There is a wealth of resources available online for supporting the teaching of primary languages, but to help you focus in on some high-quality ones we recommend the following:

- BBC Bitesize has a range of resources for Mandarin, Spanish and French –www.bbc.co.uk/bitesize
- Classics for All is a website to support the teaching of ancient languages –https://classicsforall.org.uk
- Ofsted Language Research Review – www.gov.uk/government/news/ ofsted-publishes-research-review-on-languages-education
- Primary Languages Network – https://primarylanguages.network/itt-dashboard
- Rosetta Stone resources for teachers – https://support.rosettastone.com/s/ article/resources-for-teachers?language=en_US

QUESTIONS TO ASK EXPERTS

The Initial Teacher Training Core Content Framework (DfE, 2019a) specifies that during your training you need to have input from experts. Here are some languages curriculum questions you could ask when you have the chance:

- What language do we teach children in this school? What is the rationale for this choice?
- What resources would you recommend to improve my teaching of languages?
- Can you tell me how children get better at holding conversations in language X as they move through KS2?
- How do teachers improve their subject knowledge in language X?

Discussion Questions

1 The teaching of languages is not a statutory requirement in EYFS or KS1. Do you agree or disagree with this?
2 In small groups, read the National Curriculum for Languages Key Stage 2. Choose one or two bullet points to focus on - how could this knowledge be built over time?
3 Schools may use an ancient or a modern language to study. What are the benefits of each? Are there any drawbacks?
4 Which areas of the languages curriculum do you want to learn more about to secure your subject knowledge? How will you do this, and what will you use?

16

PERSONAL, SOCIAL, HEALTH AND ECONOMIC EDUCATION (PSHE)

Why Teach PSHE to Primary Children?

Personal, social, health and economic (PSHE) education at primary level aims to teach children to make decisions in different situations that keep them safe, healthy and happy. Our education system must support pupils to gain the knowledge and understanding that prepare them for adult life. Under the umbrella of PSHE education, children will study and reflect upon different themes such as friendship, conflict, change, difference and identity. The PSHE education curriculum should prepare pupils to make informed decisions for themselves and others.

The National Curriculum does not have a programme of study for PSHE. It specifies the following:

> All schools should make provision for personal, social, health and economic education (PSHE), drawing on good practice. Schools are also free to include other subjects or topics of their choice in planning and designing their own programme of education. (DfE, 2013a: 5)

Within PSHE, there is specific guidance for one element of the curriculum: relationships education. At secondary school level, this area of the curriculum becomes sex and relationships education. It is not a requirement for primary schools to teach a programme of sex education, but it is recommended by the Department for Education. In the science curriculum, children will learn about animal, including human, reproduction. Many schools do choose to teach children in upper KS2 content that covers sex, and this will be outlined in school policy documents. It is good practice to share content with parents before it is taught to explain how it will be taught. Parents have the right to withdraw primary-aged children from lessons that contain content about sex.

During national lockdown, the Department for Education released statutory guidance for relationships education (DfE, 2021c). This was at a time when many children were at home and not able to develop and maintain relationships as they would normally. For some children, these extended periods of isolation resulted in missed developmental milestones, whilst for others it meant witnessing relationships that were understandably strained. It has always been important for children to understand how relationships work for their daily interactions with peers and for their long-term ability to foster their own positive relationships, but in the context of lockdowns and extended periods of isolation, this aspect of the primary curriculum is now more important than ever.

Many schools have included the statutory relationships content within their PSHE curriculum. Others may choose to teach it in a different way. Importantly, relationships education must be taught with a view to developing understanding and resilience to help children navigate the various challenges that life may bring.

Relationships education at primary level equips pupils with understanding in the following areas:

- family and people who care for me
- caring friendships
- respectful relationships
- online relationships
- being safe. (DfE, 2021c)

Within relationships education, an important thread of equality and respect runs throughout all content. A piece of legislation that is relevant here is the Equality Act 2010. There is specific guidance that outlines how the Equality Act impacts schools and one of the many important elements is 'protected characteristics'. This means that schools must ensure that pupils are not discriminated against because of their:

- sex
- race
- disability
- religion or belief
- sexual orientation
- gender reassignment
- pregnancy or maternity.

The PSHE curriculum is likely to be the place where content is integrated for children to learn about and understand lesbian, gay, bi-sexual and transgender identities. Individual schools determine how they approach this content but it is important that we, as teachers, know where and how children learn about LGBTQ+ within the curriculum so that we can support children's understanding of this and ensure that equality and respect are at the heart of our teaching.

There is also statutory content that covers health and mental wellbeing in the following areas:

- mental wellbeing
- internet safety and harms
- physical health and fitness
- healthy eating
- drugs, alcohol and tobacco
- health and prevention
- basic first aid
- the changing adolescent body.

The areas outlined above all contribute to a child's understanding of how to keep themselves healthy and resilient, and will support them to make informed choices in their lives. The online world is increasingly present in childhood and navigating it requires some understanding of its positive elements, but also a recognition that children are unfortunately likely to come across negative elements such as online bullying, trolling and inappropriate content. As teachers, we cannot control how children use the online world outside of school, but we can teach a robust curriculum that equips them with the knowledge, understanding and strategies to deal with the challenges of interacting with online content, including when to seek adult help with online incidents that may occur.

As we do with other subjects within our curriculum, we must consider what the journey through the PSHE education curriculum will look like for our children. How do we best introduce our children to issues they will face in their childhood? How do we develop their knowledge and skills, so that they may make informed choices that support their own health and wellbeing and that of others?

The DfE states:

> Effective teaching in these subjects will ensure that core knowledge is broken down into units of manageable size and communicated clearly to pupils, in a carefully sequenced way, within a planned programme or lessons. Teaching will include sufficient well-chosen opportunities and contexts for pupils to embed new knowledge so that it can be used confidently in real life situations. (DfE, 2019b)

As with the other primary subjects, careful sequencing of content within PSHE education is important to support the development of knowledge and skills over time. As teachers, we need to think about the vocabulary children need, which issues they will study and learn to navigate, and how we ensure the curriculum is inclusive for all children, including those with special educational needs. We might also consider how the PSHE education content fits in with school values and how an understanding of these values is embedded in and applied to different situations that children may face in their daily lives.

How Is PSHE Education Subject Knowledge Sequenced?

Sequencing subject knowledge in PSHE education simply means considering the order in which we teach content. The National Curriculum does not prescribe a precise sequence of learning for PSHE, but, as we outlined previously, there is statutory content for relationships and health, two vital aspects of PSHE education.

Many primary schools will follow a PSHE education scheme of work they have purchased, whilst others will have one they developed themselves. It is important to make sure that the content of the PSHE education curriculum we work with has sequenced content, so that knowledge and skills build over time as understanding becomes secure. Sequencing curriculum content helps us to make sure children learn and understand more over time as they encounter content in different contexts. For example, teaching children about online safety in KS1 might involve teaching children about the internet and what we use it for (watching videos, homework, playing games), and then discussing how anyone can put things on the internet and that they might not always be truthful. KS1 children may begin to learn that we must not give away personal information on the internet and that strangers may attempt to communicate with us. Then, in KS2, children might be taught more about online safety, including how to deal with online bullying, unwanted messages or photographs, spam emails, plagiarism, and securing passwords. The curriculum must develop knowledge and skills over time and must be responsive to the changing issues that children face.

Let's explore how we would sequence a Key Stage 2 unit of work in PSHE education focusing on online relationships.

What Do I Want My Children to Know and Be Able to Do at the End of This Unit?

The statutory content for Relationships Education outlines the expectations for the end of primary school. Relationships at KS2 could cover families, friends, online contacts, mental health, respect, risks, self-respect, conflict, stereotypes, boundaries, privacy, abuse, or a host of other elements. Therefore, it is important that we are specific and ensure we are teaching content in manageable chunks so children are not overloaded. This example outline will focus on online relationships, mental health and respect.

Where Will I Start?

When we embark upon planning a sequenced unit of work in PSHE education, as with other curriculum areas, we need to reconnect children to their previous learning.

You may want to ask yourself the following:

- What have children already studied in previous years? How can I connect this new learning to the previous learning? What vocabulary have they been taught before? Which situations have they focused on before?

- How can I check what children can already do and what they understand about how online relationships work? How can I find out what children understand about staying safe online?
- What can I do to support children in my class who need more support with understanding online relationships?

We then need to consider our sequence of learning: what do I want pupils to know? Which words do I want them to use confidently? Will I use any texts or videos to support their understanding? How will I check children understand what I intended them to learn? What is my end goal for this unit?

What Will My Sequence of Learning Look Like?

A sequence of learning in PSHE education will not always look the same as another, but here is an example structure:

> Step 1: Prior learning – a task to find out what children know; a quiz to check understanding of key vocabulary, including cyberbullying, anonymous, trolling, respect, virus, spam.
> Step 2: Online relationships – introduce a key text, online story, video or other resource that explores a person pretending to be someone they are not, online. Class discussion with established safe space boundaries (PSHE discussions can benefit from established rules that govern how children talk to one another, how they don't repeat or ridicule anyone for their opinions, etc). Question: Can we trust people we talk to online? Children to write a response after discussing with class/talk partners.
> Step 3: Our mental health and online relationships – explicitly teach related vocabulary, including mental health, anxiety, emotions, overwhelmed, strategy, boundary, wellbeing, support. Question: How are our online relationships and mental health linked? Discuss: How might we create boundaries for our online relationships?
> Step 4: How to keep ourselves and our friends safe – use a text, video or other resource that explores supporting a friend through a challenging online relationship. Class discussion: How might we look out for a friend who may be struggling with an online relationship? Explore how we can help our friends and what advice we might give if we notice they need our support. Discuss when to seek adult help if we are worried about a friend or an online relationship of our own.
> Step 5: Assessment task – design a guide to online friendships for a younger class.

*Steps may be one or more lessons depending on term length and timetabling.

What Does Progress Look Like Within This Unit?

Progress in primary PSHE education happens over time as children are equipped with vocabulary, knowledge and understanding in different contexts. When we look for progress in PSHE education, we are looking for children to understand the content we have taught. We can check for understanding in several ways. Checking for understanding of vocabulary is relatively straightforward and could take the form of a quiz or low-stakes test. As children progress through the lesson content, engaging with new issues or areas of PSHE education, they will be explicitly taught new vocabulary. They can then use this new vocabulary in discussions and situations they face within their own friendships, relationships and online interactions.

Understanding of concepts such as relationships or healthy living is harder to test for and checking for understanding will take the form of questioning, listening to discussions, listening to children's expression of opinions or perhaps written responses to questions. Ultimately, this area of the primary curriculum exists to prepare children for navigating life's challenges, and it is only when they apply their understanding to successfully deal with a problem, overcome a challenge or resolve a dispute, for example, that the true value of this subject will be realised.

Early Years

In the early years, PSHE has an area of learning called personal, social, emotional development (PSED). This area of learning is focused on a child's wellbeing – their sense of identity, their friendships, their feelings, their decisions and their independence. Along with physical development and communication and language, PSED is one of the three prime areas of learning in the early years. There are three Early Learning Goals within PSED used to assess children at the end of reception: self-regulation, managing self and building relationships.

Self-regulation focuses on children's understanding of their own feelings and those of others, and how children can regulate their behaviour according to these feelings. An example of this would be a child offering to help a friend who is getting frustrated because they can't find a particular toy. In this example, the child who offers to help recognises their friend's feelings of frustration and knows that, by helping, they might make their friend feel better. Another element of self-regulation is the ability to control immediate impulses when appropriate. An example of this might be joining in with nursery rhymes or songs or playing games such as grandma's footsteps. If you are singing *The wheels on the bus* with your friends, you must self-regulate to sing the right verse and to do the right actions at the right time. Self-regulation is not about complete compliance, but about making choices for your own learning or to fit in with classroom expectations. When a child walks into class, they might take off their coat and throw it on the floor, eager to start playing, or they could choose to hang up their coat on their peg before getting started. Self-regulation also involves giving attention to others, responding appropriately and following instructions.

Within the Early Learning Goal for managing self, children are expected to show confidence, independence, resilience and perseverance. An example of this could be a child trying to build a tall tower from wooden blocks; they might start building this until another child accidentally knocks it over. The child could give up, or they could persevere by deciding to start building again, choosing a different structure that doesn't fall over easily. Within managing self, children are also expected to understand the reasons for rules and to recognise right and wrong. Understanding of the concept of rules will embed over time as children learn the expectations and routines in an early years setting. Children who meet the expected level of development for managing self will also be able to manage their own basic hygiene and personal needs, such as going to the toilet and washing their hands, or making healthy choices such as eating fruit at snack time.

Finally, the third area of PSED in the early years focuses on building relationships. Children who meet the expected level of development in this area by the end of reception will be able to take turns and play cooperatively with their friends, they will form positive attachments to adults and friends, and they will show sensitivity to their own needs and those of others. A child who can do these things might be able to talk about kindness, what it means to them and how they show kindness towards others. They might know what to do to help a friend who is upset. They might help an adult to solve a problem that has arisen in the classroom.

PSED in early years focuses on the skills, awareness and development that create a strong foundation for future learning and positive experience. The PSHE education curriculum takes this learning on through KS1 and KS2 so that a child's primary education equips them with the tools they need to live, learn and grow alongside others, navigating relationships and developing a strong sense of identity.

Key Elements of the PSHE Education Curriculum

Unlike other areas of the curriculum we have explored, PSHE does not have statutory content outlined in a programme of study. It is not a statutory subject, but all schools are expected to teach it. The lack of centralised content prescribed by government means that teachers are free to develop a PSHE curriculum that meets the needs of their children. This freedom also means that the curriculum can easily be reviewed, adapted and developed in response to new challenges that children may face. For example, the online world changes very quickly and the 'online relationships' element of relationships education will need regular updates to ensure children are equipped with the correct vocabulary, knowledge and understanding they need to be resilient to challenges.

As we have established, PSHE education covers personal, social, health and economic education. There is content elsewhere in the National Curriculum that overlaps with these areas, such as areas of science that touch upon healthy eating, drugs, lifestyle choices and exercise. The 'economic' element of PSHE education at primary level touches upon an understanding of money, which is taught within the mathematics curriculum, but economics is more than just understanding how our monetary system works. Young children will be building understanding of the concept of exchange and trade from an early age, from a parent smiling at a baby and the baby smiling back, to a child wanting the blue cup that their friend has, and the friend agreeing to swap. Older children become very aware of the concept of value when collecting football cards and agreeing to trade with their friends to get the cards they want. Children might participate in bake sales or other fundraising efforts such as sponsored reads, gaining an understanding of raising money for a purpose. Self-regulation plays an important part in understanding economics: do I spend my money, or do I save it? As teachers, we can model the behaviours that show we value our belongings, our books, our classroom and our school environment. This will help children to develop an understanding of what things are worth and how we can be economically responsible, a foundation for future learning.

Relationships education, which is often taught within the PSHE curriculum, has statutory content that we explored earlier in this chapter. This content outlines the foundational learning required to recognise positive relationships within families, with other children and with adults. Children will learn about elements of positive relationships including kindness, honesty, respect and personal boundaries. Children will learn that they have rights, for example relating to their own bodies. This supports a school's role in safeguarding children; children will have a clear understanding of their own personal boundaries and will know when and how to seek help if they are concerned about inappropriate or unwanted physical contact. They will explore how friendships and relationships overlap with the online world and how to keep themselves and others safe online. Children will learn about family set-ups and the different forms they take, including but not limited to LGBTQ+ parents, adoptive parents and single-parent families.

Health education has statutory content outlined that most schools will teach within PSHE education. At primary level, this focuses on good physical health and mental wellbeing. Vital to this is the vocabulary needed to explain feelings and talk about their bodies and their own health. Children will learn about self-care in terms of personal hygiene, healthy choices, mental wellbeing and basic first aid. They will learn about the link between mental wellbeing and physical exercise, including time spent outdoors. This area of the curriculum also touches upon social interactions – hobbies, personal interests, shared activities that support overall health and wellbeing. As with the relationships content, there is an element to health education that covers online interactions and explores the impact of online contact on our mental wellbeing. This links to the self-regulation element of PSED that we explored in the early years section: when should I turn off my phone? How do I know when I've spent enough time on online gaming? Within health education, teachers will also explore poor health and wellbeing and what that includes, such as loneliness and anxiety.

Sex education is not compulsory at primary level. As we explored previously, some areas of sex education are covered within the science curriculum, such as changes from birth to old age (including puberty) and reproduction in plants and animals. Sex education, including changes in puberty, menstruation and sexual intercourse, is not compulsory, although many primary schools choose to teach a programme including this content, often in Year 5 or Year 6. Schools often consult with parents before this content is taught to ensure they are supported and are clear on what children will learn in school. Parents have the right to withdraw children from lessons including this content. Schools work alongside parents, taking account of religion, the age of the children and any special educational needs, to ensure content is appropriate.

How Do You Build Subject Knowledge?

In each of the areas covered by the National Curriculum in PSHE education, we must have the specialised *content knowledge* required to teach the subject well. We also need *pedagogical knowledge* – knowledge of how we teach PSHE in our primary classrooms.

In terms of content knowledge, when we are in school, we can explore the PSHE education curriculum the school has chosen and find out what it requires. We can explore the vocabulary, concepts and issues covered in the PSHE education curriculum and think about the misconceptions children may have. If the school teaches elements of sex education, ask if you are able to discuss their approach and look at the content taught. It may not be appropriate for you to observe these lessons, but discussing how this content is taught will be valuable. There may be pedagogical approaches that teachers use that are specific to PSHE, such as 'circle time' where children sit in a circle with well-established rules for discussions to take place. Ask subject leaders how 'safe discussion' spaces are created for certain aspects of PSHE education.

It is our responsibility to recognise our own knowledge gaps and fill them by reading and researching. What we need to know within PSHE will depend on which age group we are teaching, but at this early stage whilst training, it is important for us to familiarise ourselves with the content we may be required to teach. Make use of resources such as subject associations and guidance that may come with your school's PSHE education curriculum.

Summary

What we have discussed in this chapter:

- Primary PSHE education prepares children for navigating life; for relationships, health, changes and challenges.
- A high-quality PSHE education curriculum is well sequenced and clearly identifies what the children will learn from EYFS to Key Stage 2. This clarity helps teachers to teach effective lessons and helps children to learn, remember and be able to do more over time.
- Our own knowledge of both PSHE education subject content (what we teach) and pedagogy (how we teach) is crucial and will develop throughout our teaching career.

Signposts to Additional Resources

Exploring these resources will deepen your understanding of the role of PSHE education in the primary curriculum:

- Little Parachutes is a website that suggests picture books that tackle issues children face such as anxiety, friendship problems, self-esteem, body changes and new beginnings; there are many suggestions here that would support teaching of the PSHE education curriculum – www.littleparachutes.com
- PSHE Association – https://pshe-association.org.uk
- Relationships and sex education and health education, DfE – www.gov.uk/government/publications/relationships-education-relationships-and-sex-education-rse-and-health-education
- Young Minds is the UK's leading charity promoting the mental health of children and young people – www.youngminds.org.uk

QUESTIONS TO ASK EXPERTS

The Initial Teacher Training Core Content Framework (DfE, 2019a) specifies that during your training you need to have input from experts. Here are some PSHE education curriculum questions you could ask when you have the chance:

- Can you help me to understand how the PSHE education curriculum is structured?
- What materials are available to help me prepare my lessons?
- What resources can I use to improve my own subject knowledge?
- What do we expect children in the year I am working in to understand in PSHE?

Discussion Questions

1 In small groups, read the Early Learning Goals for Personal, Social, Emotional Development. Discuss what self-regulation might look like in the early years.

2 In small groups, read the National Curriculum statutory content for Relationships and Health in primary school. How do knowledge and skills build over time?

3 How can we help our pupils to navigate the online world safely?

4 Which areas of PSHE education do you want to learn more about to secure your subject knowledge? How will you do this, and what resources will you use?

17

COMPUTING

Why Teach Computing to Primary Children?

'Everyone in this country should learn how to program because it teaches you how to think.' (Steve Jobs) sites.ed.gov/whhbcu/multimedia/everyone-in-this-country-should-learn-how-to-program-because-it-teaches-you-how-to-think-steve-jobs/#:~:text=HBCU%20Scholar%20Cohort-,%E2%80%9CEveryone%20 in%20this%20country%20should%20learn%20how%20to%20program%20 because,how%20to%20think%E2%80%9D%20%E2%80%93%20Steve%20Jobs

When the 2014 National Curriculum was introduced, one of the major changes was the introduction of the subject of 'computing' (we had previously taught Information and Communication Technology), with a greater emphasis on teaching children computer science. The justification for this is outlined in the purpose of study for computing, which states:

Computing also ensures that pupils become digitally literate – able to use, and express themselves and develop their ideas through information and communication technology – at a level suitable for the future workplace and as active participants in a digital world.

As the curriculum rightly states, we live in a digital world and we need to prepare our children to be successful in this world. Technology is constantly evolving and it is a fundamental part of our daily lives – we use it to communicate with each other, find directions, work, educate and much more, so it is essential our children have a good grounding in computing. We also know that many job opportunities require a level of computational thinking, so by providing our children with a curriculum which develops computational thinking, we are preparing them for their future job prospects.

Whilst there are endless benefits to the advancements in technology, we only need to read the news daily to understand the risks associated with the internet. We want our children to be able to use the internet and technology safely, so we need to teach them how to mitigate potential harmful situations and how to respond to these when they occur. By teaching e-safety as part of our computing lessons, we are supporting children to use technology in a safer and healthier manner.

In May 2022, Ofsted published its research review into computing (Ofsted, 2022b). Like all of the organisation's research reviews, they can be read in full on the Ofsted website and we would recommend you do this. However, some of the key points from the research which might support your thinking as a trainee teacher are outlined below:

- When considering progression in computing, you should consider this via three aspects of computing: computer science, information technology and digital literacy. You are able to group all the curriculum statements to fall under one of these headings and this will help you consider how a pupil progresses.
- Computer science should be planned sequentially in the curriculum so that children become better at programming in a logical manner.
- The use of digital artefacts should be planned meaningfully within the curriculum.
- Do not assume that pupils are already experts in digital literacy because they have grown up with technology around them; they should be considered as novices to ensure they are taught all aspects of the curriculum.
- E-safety should be taught in a sequenced manner so that children gain age-appropriate content. (Ofsted, 2022b)

How Is Computing Subject Knowledge Sequenced?

Sequencing subject knowledge in computing means thinking carefully about the order in which we teach things. As you will see later in this chapter, the content in the National Curriculum for computing is quite specific, but there is not much detail included about how we might sequence the curriculum for children to achieve the end of key stage outcomes in small steps.

The order in which our curriculum content is taught matters. Although there may not be a consensus, no perfect way in which to order the knowledge in the computing curriculum, thinking about sequencing helps us to break down what we want to teach into small, manageable chunks. Some schools may purchase a scheme to support with the teaching of computing, but you will still need to adapt this to meet the needs of your class and ensure the activities and learning set out in the scheme are as good as you want them to be.

Let us now have a look at an aspect of the Key Stage 1 computing curriculum and consider how we might sequence this aspect. By the end of this key stage, children should be able to debug simple programs. You would teach this across Year 1 and Year 2 to provide children with opportunities to learn the foundations they need first, and then revisit and build upon this learning throughout the key stage.

Where Will I Start?

For me to teach debugging, children will need to have wider computing experience first; they can then develop their experience of creating simple programs. I will therefore need to ensure that children have a secure understanding of algorithms and have experience of creating some short programs. I will check pupils' existing knowledge and ensure they have a secure understanding. I will use the same software children have already been using to create their programs and algorithms (your school will have specific software or a type of floor robot).

What Will My Sequence of Learning Look Like?

I will break down the knowledge content so that I am introducing new knowledge in small manageable chunks. My sequence of learning may look like this:

Step 1: Reconnect to prior learning – recap and build on what knowledge children have already learnt in relation to creating programs. I would ensure children understand the importance of providing unambiguous instructions when designing a program, and how these instructions are connected in a sequence.

Step 2: I will revisit and build upon their knowledge of algorithms. I will introduce a floor robot for children to create simple algorithms, and the children will develop their understanding by changing the order of a sequence to see what happens.

Step 3: Children will design and create their own larger programming project which will require them to introduce different algorithms in the different parts of the project. It will be at this point that I introduce 'debugging'. I will model to the children the process of finding and fixing errors within an algorithm and a program, and explain to the children that we call this process 'debugging' in computing. I will explain that this is a small but very important component within programming, and encourage children to articulate what they have debugged in their design and to use the correct vocabulary.

*Steps may require one lesson or more than one, especially step 3.

What Does Progress Look Like Within This Unit?

When we look for progress, we look for a number of things under the umbrella of 'knowing more and being able to do more'. For the example given here, you will notice that debugging features as part of a much wider unit on programming, but if I wanted to specifically consider the progress made in debugging, I would consider the following:

- Children using the correct vocabulary when discussing errors will demonstrate progress.
- When creating their programs, I would be able to observe whether children are becoming more proficient in both their ability to solve problems which arise within their design and to predict any potential errors that may arise.
- By providing children with opportunities to reflect on their design, I might ask targeted questions such as, 'Is there something you debugged which you have learnt from?', to check pupils' understanding.
- I might purposefully plan algorithms which need to be debugged to share with the children to check their understanding.

When sequencing our curriculum content, we should think about what children have already learned, what we want them to learn and where they will take their learning next. It is helpful to familiarise yourself with the expectations for the previous year and for the year following the one you are teaching in.

Early Years

Within the EYFS, there is no direct reference to computing itself but, as part of the Understanding the World programme of study, it states that children should 'foster their understanding of our culturally, socially, technologically and ecologically diverse world' and that it is up to individual schools to decide how they might teach this to children in their EYFS.

Whilst computing and technology receive little reference in the early years framework, that does not mean they do not feature largely within many EYFS environments – in fact, the EYFS baseline, which is the statutory requirement for all reception children, is completed using a tablet device. Often, technology is an effective tool to teach other aspects of the curriculum and to set the foundations for KS1. Some ways you might see technology incorporated within an EYFS curriculum are as follows:

- teaching the children how to use technology for recording photographs so that they can make close observations, such as the changing of seasons over the year
- using video recording when children are role-playing/retelling familiar stories, which will support their communication and language
- using the internet to look at the local area/maps to develop children's sense of space
- some teachers using technology to support their assessment, e.g. recording/ taking photos of pupil outcomes
- children being taught how to use technology safely.

Key Elements of the Computing Curriculum

The computing curriculum does not take up much space in the National Curriculum document – in fact, it is only two pages! Whilst this might not sound like much, the four aims set out by the National Curriculum ensure all pupils:

- can understand and apply the fundamental principles and concepts of computer science, including abstraction, logic, algorithms and data representation
- can analyse problems in computational terms, and have repeated practical experience of writing computer programs in order to solve such problems
- can evaluate and apply information technology, including new or unfamiliar technologies, analytically, to solve problems
- are responsible, competent, confident and creative users of information and communication technology. (DfE, 2013a)

As you can see, the aims are quite specific about what the children should know and the curriculum further breaks the subject content down into key stages.

In Key Stage 1, pupils should be taught to:

- understand what algorithms are; how they are implemented as programs on digital devices; and that programs execute by following precise and unambiguous instructions

- create and debug simple programs
- use logical reasoning to predict the behaviour of simple programs
- use technology purposefully to create, organise, store, manipulate and retrieve digital content
- recognise common uses of information technology beyond school
- use technology safely and respectfully, keeping personal information private; and to identify where to go for help and support when they have concerns about content or contact on the internet or other online technologies.

In Key Stage 2, pupils should be taught to:

- design, write and debug programs that accomplish specific goals, including controlling or simulating physical systems; solve problems by decomposing them into smaller parts
- use sequence, selection and repetition in programs; work with variables and various forms of input and output
- use logical reasoning to explain how some simple algorithms work and to detect and correct errors in algorithms and programs
- understand computer networks including the internet; how they can provide multiple services, such as the World Wide Web; and the opportunities they offer for communication and collaboration
- use search technologies effectively, appreciate how results are selected and ranked, and be discerning in evaluating digital content
- select, use and combine a variety of software (including internet services) on a range of digital devices to design and create a range of programs, systems and content that accomplish given goals, including collecting, analysing, evaluating and presenting data and information
- use technology safely, respectfully and responsibly; to recognise acceptable/ unacceptable behaviour; and to identify a range of ways to report concerns about content and contact. (DfE, 2013a)

The content above is what children should have been taught by the time they finish that key stage. Whilst what is captured in a few bullet points is quite specific, it is up to individual schools to design a curriculum which enables pupils to achieve these end of key stage statements as the curriculum does not provide this information. As mentioned earlier, this requires schools to consider what smaller steps and what core knowledge children will need to learn in a way that supports progression. It is not unusual for staff to purchase a ready-made computing scheme which they will implement in their school. Where a school does this, it must ensure the scheme is successfully enabling children to achieve the aims of the National Curriculum, and, as a teacher, you will need to quality-assure the lessons are right for your children.

Depending on your confidence in using IT and your familiarity with some of the terminology used within the computing curriculum, it can feel daunting when you first look at the large scale of knowledge required to teach this subject. At the end of the chapter, you will be able to avail of some additional resources to support you with teaching computing, and we will also discuss how to build your own subject knowledge, but some key aspects of the curriculum are highlighted below:

- Using technology safely: The computing curriculum recognises that it is essential to learn computing and there are many benefits to this, however we only need to look at the media almost daily to be aware of the risks that can be associated with technology, and we have a duty to teach children in primary school about being safe when using technology. All computing curricula will have a strand on e-safety and children should be taught this regularly – especially as the risks continually evolve depending on the latest apps and developments with technology. Your school may celebrate Safer Internet Day as part of its curriculum and it is likely e-safety is also taught within your school's PSHE curriculum. You should speak with your school's computing lead to find out whether the school has an e-safety policy and how children are taught to use technology safely.
- Computer science: At the heart of computing is computer science, which the National Curriculum describes thus: 'pupils are taught the principles of information and computation, how digital systems work, and how to put this knowledge to use through programming'. Pupils in both KS1 and KS2 will learn about algorithms and debugging – is this something you are confident teaching? How will you explain what this terminology means to children? Many schools use specific software to teach these aspects of the curriculum (e.g. Scratch) which you should practise using to build your own confidence.
- Being digitally literate: We know that we use technology to communicate and share information as part of daily life. It is therefore important that our children are digitally literate as it is highly likely that it is a skill they will need for the remainder of their lives. Children need to learn how to be digitally literate safely and to understand how to communicate effectively using technology – we also want them to be aware of any potential signs of communication which might not be genuine.

How Do You Build Subject Knowledge?

As with all curriculum subjects, we all have different starting points, and you need to be aware of what gaps might exist within your own subject knowledge so you can teach it effectively. The National Curriculum for computing should be your starting point for assessing your own subject knowledge – read what the curriculum outlines, and highlight what you feel you have secure subject knowledge in and what you need to develop. The subject knowledge audit in the appendix will provide you with some specific aspects of the curriculum to reflect upon.

When you read the primary computing curriculum, you will notice the specific language used throughout and one key area will be to ensure you understand and can explain the meaning of this language. For example, 'algorithm' is a word we need to teach children in both KS1 and KS2 – we need to ensure we understand what this word means, how we might explain the meaning confidently to children and how we might teach the children algorithms. In order to develop your subject knowledge in this aspect, you might consider looking at a glossary from the Computing Hub website (see the additional resources section at the end of the chapter) to ensure your understanding is accurate. You should also check what curriculum materials your school uses to teach algorithms and that you are confident using these materials to support your explanations of algorithms. You might consider scripting your explanations before you directly teach the children.

As well as content knowledge, you will need to ensure you are confident in your pedagogical knowledge (how best to teach computing). There are many unique aspects to the teaching of computing which do not exist in the other disciplines, and as a teacher you need to ensure that you consider all these aspects when teaching this subject. Some points for you to consider are outlined below:

- Where will I deliver my computing lessons? Is there a computing room I can use? Does the school have a set of laptops to deliver lessons in the main classroom? Do I need to use tablets to deliver this lesson? Is this a lesson that does not require the children to use any physical technology? It is important that we have a clear understanding of the above as this will dictate how we manage behaviour; how we deploy additional adults; how we plan to troubleshoot problems (e.g. batteries in tablets not being charged); and how we ensure inclusion for all.
- If I need to use specific software to deliver a session, I will need to ensure I am expert enough when using this software so I can model for the children what is expected.
- How will I give an opportunity to reconnect to prior learning? For example, revisiting the technical language taught, showing a common mistake/misconception previously taught and asking the children to correct it, or specifically reminding the children what they learnt in the last lesson(s).
- How will I explicitly teach the key vocabulary? As computing lessons will often have specific vocabulary, script how you will explain the meanings and what key questions you will ask to check for understanding.

- Consider how I will manage behaviour when children are using technology, so that I can get their full attention when needed. When I first bring children to a computing room/introduce devices, make it clear what my expectations are so that I don't waste time managing behaviour which I can counter at the start.
- Once I have identified what I want the children to learn in computing, how will I break it down into small, manageable chunks, ensuring children are not overloaded? What am I saying? What am I showing the children? Are they listening, watching, reading, and is that what I want them to do? How am I modelling using technology effectively?
- What teaching resources will I use to support children's learning? For example, devices, software, STEM resources.

Summary

We have discussed in this chapter:

- It is critical that children become digitally literate for the world we live in.
- A high-quality computing curriculum begins in the EYFS and is built sequentially across KS1 and KS2.
- It is essential that we teach our children to be safe when using technology.
- We need to have secure subject knowledge as teachers and a range of resources are available to help us with this.

Signposts to Additional Resources

Like all subjects, there is a plethora of resources available to support the teaching of computing. Some of the resources we would advise you to consider can be found below:

- Barefoot Computing offers resources and training which can support teachers to teach computing well – www.barefootcomputing.org
- Computing Hubs is a great resource to develop your knowledge of computing; the organisation offers a range of courses and resources. You can find your local computing hub here – https://teachcomputing.org/hubs
- STEM provides resources which support the teaching of computing – www. stem.org.uk/primary/resources/collections/computing
- Teach Computing has some useful resources to support the teaching of the primary curriculum – https://teachcomputing.org/curriculum

━━━━━━━━ QUESTIONS TO ASK EXPERTS ━━━━━━━━

When meeting with experts, some questions you could ask them include:

- How is the computing curriculum developed and sequenced from EYFS to Year 6?
- What advice would you give me to ensure my subject knowledge is secure?
- How do children develop their understanding of algorithms in KS1 and KS2?
- How is e-safety taught? What are some of the most challenging aspects of teaching e-safety?
- What resources do you use to teach computer science?

Discussion Questions

1 The National Curriculum for Computing requires us to teach children how to use technology safely. Some people might feel that the risks of technology outweigh the benefits. Discuss this in small groups.

2 In small groups, read the National Curriculum aims for KS1 and KS2. Focus on one of these aims and discuss what children would need to know to achieve this aim.

3 Which areas of computing do you want to learn more about to secure your subject knowledge? How will you do this?

Appendix 1: Primary Subject Knowledge Audit

This subject knowledge audit highlights key knowledge from the primary curriculum and provides a starting point for a new teacher. It aims to provide a useful baseline for the different disciplines you are required to teach. It is obviously not an exhaustive list of everything primary teachers need to know, but it helps to identify gaps in subject knowledge.

Early Reading - Phonics

	NO	YES
Secure knowledge of the phonics scheme used by school		
All 40 phonemes		
Alternative sounds for graphemes		
Common exception words		
Grapheme-phoneme correspondences (GPCs)		

Reading - Comprehension

	NO	YES
10 children's authors		
5 children's poets		
Different forms of poetry		
Different forms of fiction		
Different forms of non-fiction		
3 tiers of vocabulary and what they mean		

Writing - Including Spelling and Handwriting

	NO	YES
Vowel digraphs and trigraphs		
Compound words		
Use of the apostrophe		
Homophones		
Prefix and suffix		
Use of the hyphen		
Noun phrase		
Determiner		
Relative clause and pronoun		
Parenthesis		
Synonym and antonym		
Adverbial		
Correct pen grip		
Different tenses		
Dialogue in writing		

Maths

	NO	YES
Fractions		
Ratios and proportions		
Decimals		
Percentages		
Basic operations		
Measurement		
Data and statistics		

Science

	NO	YES
Seed dispersal		
Germination		
Pollination		
Photosynthesis		
Food chains		
Vertebrates and invertebrates		
Amphibians, fish, reptiles, mammals and birds		
Carnivores, omnivores and herbivores		
Micro-organisms		
Life cycles		
Adaptation		
Properties of solids, liquids and gases		
Simple circuits		
Properties of magnets		
Practical scientific methods for working scientifically		

Art

	NO	YES
5 great artists (modern and historical)		
3 great architects and designers		
Primary and secondary colours		
2 sculpting techniques		
2 sketching techniques		
1 printing technique		

Computing

	NO	YES
Explain meaning of programming		
Explain meaning of algorithm		
Explain meaning of coding		
Explain meaning of debugging		
How children stay safe online		

Design & Technology

	NO	YES
3 tools which can be used to perform practical tasks (e.g. cutting, shaping, joining and finishing)		
2 different mechanisms		
Principles of a healthy and varied diet		

Geography KS1&2

	NO	YES
Seven continents and five oceans		
Equator		
Compass points		
Northern and Southern Hemispheres		
Climate zones		
Settlements		
Water cycle		
River formation		
Volcanoes		
Earthquakes		
Using an atlas		
Using a range of maps		
Examples of physical features		
Examples of human features		

History (Through History Unit You Are Teaching, e.g. Ancient Egypt)

	NO	YES
Chronology: Timeline of events		
Early civilisations		
Themes in British history		
Significant historical events, people and places in your school's locality		
Primary and secondary sources		

Languages KS2 (Specific to Language Taught in Your School)

	NO	YES
Speak in simple sentences		
Write simple sentences		
Know at least 1 song and rhyme (if relevant)		

Music

	NO	YES
3 great composers/musicians		
Pitch		
Rhythm		
Pulse		
Tempo		
Timbre		

PE

	NO	YES
3 attacking and defending in team games		
3 balance movements in gymnastics		
3 pieces of apparatus and their use		
3 dance movements		

RE

	NO	YES
Key symbols for the six major religions		
Holy books for the six major religions		
Places of worship for the six major religions		
Key events/celebrations for the six major religions		
Key beliefs of the six major religions		

End of KS2 Assessments

End of KS2 - Reading

You will find links to the end of the KS2 reading assessment here – www.gov.uk/government/publications/key-stage-2-tests-2019-english-reading-test-materials

This will provide you with a good understanding of what standard of texts children should be reading at the end of KS2. To reach the expected standard, children need to be scoring about 30 marks, and to reach the higher standard they need to be scoring about 40+ marks.

Explore the Mark Scheme of one of the papers. Is there anything which you need to develop within your own subject knowledge?

Actions Identified:

End of KS2 - English Grammar and Punctuation

You will find links to the end of the KS2 grammar and punctuation assessment here – www.gov.uk/government/publications/key-stage-2-tests-2019-english-grammar-punctuation-and-spelling-test-materials

This will provide you with a good understanding of what standard of grammar and spelling knowledge children should have at the end of KS2. To reach the expected standard, children need to be scoring about 40 marks, and to reach the higher standard they need to be scoring about 58+ marks.

Explore the Mark Scheme of one of the papers. Is there anything which you need to develop within your own subject knowledge?

Actions Identified:

End of KS2 - Writing Exemplification

You will find links to moderated writing at the end of KS2 here – www.gov.uk/government/publications/2018-teacher-assessment-exemplification-ks2-english-writing

You will find examples of writing which has been agreed as working at Age-Related standards and at Higher standard. Review the writing and the explanations as to why the writing is judged at Age-Related or better. Is there anything you need to improve on?

Actions Identified:

Actions and Development

Half Term 1

	Area of focus	Actions	Evaluation (including next steps)
1			
2			
3			

Half Term 2

	Area of focus	Actions	Evaluation (including next steps)
1			
2			
3			

Half Term 3

	Area of focus	Actions	Evaluation (including next steps)
1			
2			
3			

Half Term 4

	Area of focus	Actions	Evaluation (including next steps)
1			
2			
3			

Half Term 5

	Area of focus	Actions	Evaluation (including next steps)
1			
2			
3			

Half Term 6

	Area of focus	Actions	Evaluation (including next steps)
1			
2			
3			

Glossary

Alphabetic code: This refers to the correspondence between phonemes and the actual letters which represent these phonemes.

Curriculum: Everything that is taught in a school, structured and sequenced over time.

Disciplinary knowledge: Knowledge of how, within a discipline, knowledge is established, for instance how scientists establish facts.

Diversity: The representation of many different identities and differences, including, but not limited to, race, ethnicity, gender, disability, sexual orientation, and nationality.

Early Years Foundation Stage: An outline of the standards for learning, development and care of children from birth to age 5. The foundation stage curriculum is followed in nursery and reception.

Grapheme: A written letter or letters that make a single sound.

Inclusion: An education that includes everyone and reflects diversity.

Key Stage: The National Curriculum is divided into four key stages: Key Stage 1 (Years 1 and 2), Key Stage 2 (Years 3–6), both within primary school; Key Stage 3 (Years 7–9) and Key Stage 4 (Years 10–11), both within secondary school.

National Curriculum: A set of subjects and standards, published by the Department for Education, used by schools to ensure children are taught foundational knowledge.

Pedagogy: The methods of teaching, the 'how' we teach.

Phoneme: A single sound.

Phonics: An approach to early reading that teaches children the sounds in our language and the letters that are used to represent those sounds.

Programme of study: The prescribed syllabus that must be taught at each key stage.

Sequencing: Putting things in an order; in the context of the curriculum, this means ordering curriculum content to support children to learn and remember more over time.

Substantive knowledge: Within a discipline, that which is held to be true; the knowledge that teachers teach as established fact.

References

Bianchi, L., Whittaker, C. and Poole, A. (2021) *The 10 key issues with children's learning in primary science in England*. Manchester: University of Manchester/The Ogden Trust. Available at: https://documents.manchester.ac.uk/display.aspx?DocID=57599 (accessed 27/01/23).

Bruer. Available at: https://mathsnoproblem.com/en/approach/concrete-pictorial-abstract/

Crofton, I. and Fraser, D. (1985) *A Dictionary of Musical Quotations*. London: Macmillan.

Department for Education (DfE) (2011) *Teachers' standards*. London: DfE. Available at: www.gov.uk/government/publications/teachers-standards (accessed 27/01/23).

Department for Education (DfE) (2012) *Research evidence on reading for pleasure*. London: DfE. Available at: https://assets.publishing.service.gov.uk/government/uploads/system/uploads/attachment_data/file/284286/reading_for_pleasure.pdf (accessed 27/01/23).

Department for Education (DfE) (2013a) *The national curriculum in England: Primary curriculum*. London: DfE. Available at: www.gov.uk/government/publications/national-curriculum-in-england-primary-curriculum (accessed 27/01/23).

Department for Education (DfE) (2013b) *The national curriculum in England: Music programmes of study*. London: DfE. Available at: www.gov.uk/government/publications/national-curriculum-in-england-music-programmes-of-study (accessed 27/01/23).

Department for Education (DfE) (2013c) *History programmes of study: Key stages 1 and 2 national curriculum in England*. London: DfE. Available at: https://assets.publishing.service.gov.uk/government/uploads/system/uploads/attachment_data/file/239035/PRIMARY_national_curriculum_-_History.pdf (accessed 27/01/23).

Department for Education (DfE) (2015) *National curriculum in England: Science programmes of study*. London: DfE. Available at: www.gov.uk/government/publications/national-curriculum-in-england-science-programmes-of-study/national-curriculum-in-england-science-programmes-of-study (accessed 27/01/23).

Department for Education (DfE) (2019a) *Initial teacher training (ITT): Core content framework*. London: DfE. Available at: www.gov.uk/government/publications/initial-teacher-training-itt-core-content-framework (accessed 27/01/23).

Department for Education (DfE) (2019b) *Statutory guidance: Relationships and sex education (RSE) and health education*. London: DfE. Available at: www.gov.uk/

government/publications/relationships-education-relationships-and-sex-education-rse-and-health-education (accessed 27/01/23).

Department for Education (DfE) (2021a) *Early years foundation stage (EYFS) statutory framework*. London: DfE. Available at: www.gov.uk/government/publications/early-years-foundation-stage-profile-handbook (accessed 27/01/23).

Department for Education (DfE) (2021b) *Model music curriculum: Key stages 1 to 3*. London: DfE. Available at: https://assets.publishing.service.gov.uk/government/uploads/system/uploads/attachment_data/file/974366/Model_Music_Curriculum_Full.pdf (accessed 27/01/23).

Department for Education (DfE) (2021c) *Statutory guidance: Relationships education (primary)*. London: DfE. Available at: www.gov.uk/government/publications/relationships-education-relationships-and-sex-education-rse-and-health-education/relationships-education-primary (accessed 27/01/23).

Department for Education (DfE) (2022a) *The reading framework: Teaching the foundations of literacy*. London: DfE. Available at: www.gov.uk/government/publications/the-reading-framework-teaching-the-foundations-of-literacy (accessed 27/01/23).

Department for Education (DfE) (2022b) *The early years foundation stage profile 2023 handbook*. London: DfE. Available at: https://assets.publishing.service.gov.uk/government/uploads/system/uploads/attachment_data/file/1109972/Early_Years_Foundation_Stage_profile_2023_handbook.pdf (accessed 27/01/23).

Doull, K. (2022) *Teaching a Diverse Primary Curriculum*. Exeter: Learning Matters.

Education Endowment Foundation (EEF) (2020) *Improving literacy in key stage 1*. London: EEF. Available at: https://educationendowmentfoundation.org.uk/education-evidence/guidance-reports/literacy-ks-1 (accessed 27/01/23).

Education Endowment Foundation (EEF) (2021) *Improving mathematics in the early years and key stage 1*. London: EEF. Available at: https://educationendowment-foundation.org.uk/education-evidence/guidance-reports/early-maths (accessed 27/01/23).

Education Endowment Foundation (EEF) (2022) *Improving mathematics in key stages 2 and 3*. London: EEF. Available at: https://educationendowmentfoundation.org.uk/education-evidence/guidance-reports/maths-ks-2-3 (accessed 27/01/23).

Guardian, The (2016) Interview: David Olusoga: 'There's a dark side to British history, and we saw a flash of it this summer', 4 November. Available at: www.theguardian.com/books/2016/nov/04/david-olusoga-interview-black-history (accessed 27/01/23).

Hart, B. and Risley, T.R. (2003) 'The early catastrophe: The 30 million word gap by age 3', *American Educator*, 27(1): 4–9.

Hirsch, E.D. (2006) *The Knowledge Deficit: Closing the Shocking Education Gap for American Children*. Boston, MA: Houghton Mifflin.

Law, J., Charlton, J. and Asmussen, K. (2017) *Language as a child wellbeing indicator*. London: Early Intervention Foundation. Available at: www.eif.org.uk/report/language-as-a-child-wellbeing-indicator (accessed 27/01/23).

M. Hunter. (2015) *The Design Council*. Available at: www.designcouncil.org.uk/our-resources/framework-for-innovation/

Newton, I. (1675) Letter to Robert Hooke, 5 February.

Obama, B. (2012) National Geographic GeoBee. Available at: https://education.nationalgeographic.org/resource/edu-obama-question/

Ofsted (2021a) *Research review series: Mathematics*. London: Ofsted. Available at: www. gov.uk/government/publications/research-review-series-mathematics (accessed 27/01/23).

Ofsted (2021b) *Research review series: Geography*. London: Ofsted. Available at: www. gov.uk/government/publications/research-review-series-geography (accessed 27/01/23).

Ofsted (2021c) *Research review series: Languages*. London: Ofsted. Available at: www. gov.uk/government/publications/curriculum-research-review-series-languages (accessed 27/01/23).

Ofsted (2022a) *Research review series: PE*. London: Ofsted. Available at: www.gov.uk/government/publications/research-review-series-pe/research-review-series-pe (accessed 27/01/23).

Ofsted (2022b) *Research review series: Computing*. London: Ofsted. Available at: www. gov.uk/government/publications/research-review-series-computing (accessed 27/01/23).

Standards and Testing Agency (STA) (2019) *Key stage 2 science sampling 2018: Methodology note and outcomes*. London: STA. Available at: https://assets.publishing. service.gov.uk/government/uploads/system/uploads/attachment_data/file/818678/ Key_stage_2_science_sampling_2018_methodology_note_and_outcomes.pdf (accessed 27/01/23).

The Parliament Post (2021) Available at: https://post.parliament.uk/research-briefings/ post-pn-0640/

Vogelsang, M., Vogelsang, L., Diamond, S. and Sinha, P. (2022) 'Prenatal auditory experience and its sequelae', *Developmental Science*, e13278.

Wellcome Trust (2017) *State of the nation report of UK primary science education.* London: Wellcome Trust. Available at: https://wellcome.ac.uk/reports/state-nationreport-uk-primary-science-education (accessed 27/01/23).

Wellcome Trust (2020) *Evaluation of the primary science campaign*. London: Wellcome Trust. Available at: https://wellcome.org/sites/default/files/evaluation-of-the-primary-science-campaign-2020.pdf (accessed 27/01/23).

Youth Sport Trust (2021) *Primary PE activities*. Available at: www.youthsporttrust.org/ resources/physical-challenges-for-kids/primary-pe-activities (accessed 27/01/23).

Index

Note- Page number with '*f*' indicates figure, '*t*' indicates table.